Flowers On The Path

Flowers On The Path

ISBN No: 81-87910-05-4

Published by: **Isha Foundation**
15, Govindasamy Naidu Layout
Singanallur, Coimbatore - 641 005 INDIA

Phone: +91-422-2515345
E-Mail: info@ishafoundation.org
Web: ishafoundation.org

First Edition: Isha Gramotsavam 2007, Chennai
Second Edition: Mahashivarathri - March 2008

Flowers On The Path

SADHGURU

ISHA FOUNDATION

Contents

Everyday Flowers

Flowers On The Path

Flowers Of The Beyond

Introduction

The flower has kindled the human imagination in various ways. Poets and paramours, mystics and minstrels have invoked it as a richly multivalent symbol. Its subtlety and fragrance, its delicacy and transience, its mysterious self-containment and exuberant beauty, have made it an enduring source of wonder. Despite being the stuff of song and scripture, lyric and legend for centuries, it refuses – obstinately – to flatten into cliche.

The classic metaphor of "the lotus in the marsh" continues to be a powerful reminder of how to be in this world but not of it. It startles one into the sudden awareness that it is possible, despite the odds, to transform squalor into beauty, dross into refinement. The "lilies of the field" remain an evocative symbol of a natural and effortless grace, reminding us that utility and beauty, work and play, need not be mutually exclusive. The Buddhist tradition tells us of the Silent Sermon in which the Buddha simply held up a flower and gazed at it. After some time, the monk, Mahakashyapa, began to smile. He was the only monk who understood.

Yogic lore has used flower symbolism extensively. The human spine is likened to a stem and the brain to its flower. The stem requires painstaking and unfaltering care, without which the "flowering" of the mind would be impossible. There are also milestones on the path that help the seeker-gardener ascertain her/his progress. For the various chakras or energy centers in the body are also described as flowers that blossom when they are activated. Thus the entire spiritual journey is mapped out in terms of floral imagery.

The ultimate goal, or the zenith of the spiritual process, is described – in a well-known image – as the flowering of human conciousness, the unfurling of the Sahasrara, the thousand-petaled lotus. And when after a long struggle, the seeker decides – either out of desperation or wisdom – to put down the baggage of sole proprietorship, it is at the "lotus feet" of the Guru.

Flowers, for Sadhguru, have always been special. Wherever he is, flowers are seldom far away. There is nothing flamboyant about their presence. But in their own quiet way, they add something ineffable but distinctive to the ambience. And for all his robust logic and commonsense, there is something about his utterances that cannot be decoded by rationality alone. A sathsang with him is not mere fodder for the intellect; instead, it leaves many with the sense of having inhaled something elusive, tantalizing, unnamable. And so perhaps those flowers that surround him work on a more figurative level as well.

The *Flowers On The Path* series is a bouquet. It comprises articles created by Sadhguru for the *Speaking Tree* column of the *Times of India*. These articles have, for many years, brought daily infusions of beauty, humor, clarity and wisdom into lives abraded by mayhem and monotony. In pages devoted to the changing weather of the stock market and international affairs, these articles have brought readers moments of unexpected insight and stillness.

Sadhguru's original thoughts, outspoken comments and references to current affairs have sometimes provoked controversy. But they have invariably added vitality and color to a national debate.

Like flowers, these articles have inspired and stimulated readers, wafting into their lives as a gentle fragrance on some mornings, and on others, startling them awake with fresh perspectives on age-old ideas and beliefs.

And like flowers, they are essentially invitations. Invitations to follow a scent. A scent that teases, maddens and intoxicates. A scent that reminds one that life at its deepest is not a puzzle to be solved, but a mystery to be experienced.

This book is an invitation to follow that scent to its very source.

– Arundhathi Subramaniam

Everyday Flowers

 # Health Is Wholeness

Right now, medical sciences are limited to just knowing the physical body. If anything happens beyond that, you think it's a miracle.

Fundamentally, the word health itself comes from the root word "whole". What we call, "feeling healthy," is that we have a sense of wholeness within us. If we are free of diseases medically, that is not health. If we feel like a complete human being in our body, mind and spirit, that is when we are really healthy. There are any number of people who are medically healthy, but not healthy in the real sense because they do not experience a sense of wellness within themselves.

If one has to experience this sense of wholeness and oneness, it's important that one's body, mind, and above all, one's energy functions in a certain level of intensity within oneself. Now, physically, as per medical terms, one may be healthy, but the energies may be lethargic. One doesn't know why things don't happen in life the way they should, both inside and outside; this is simply because one is not taking care of the well-being of one's energy.

For every physical or psychological situation that you go through in life, there is an energy basis, which in turn has a chemical basis. In a way, modern allopathic medicines have become just chemistry. For every problem that arises in your body, you are just trying to take in some medicine, a chemical, and come to some kind of balance. If you use one chemical to bring down one aspect, or enhance another, there is also a side effect to this. For this side effect, there is an antidote; for the antidote there is another antidote; it's an endless chain.

Health Is Wholeness

Whatever is happening on the chemistry level in your body is only controlled by the way your energies function. Because a man has got excess acids within him, you instill some alkaline medicine into him. But why does he have excessive acids? Because of the way his mind, his body, and above all, his energy, functions.

So, in yoga, when we say health, we don't look at the body; we don't look at the mind; we only look at the way the energy is. If your energy body is in proper balance and full flow, your physical body and mental body will be in perfect health. There is no question about it. Keeping the energy body in full flow is not about doing any kind of healing or things like that. This is about going to the foundations of your energy system and activating it in a proper way, building a foundational yogic practice that establishes your energy in such a way that your body and mind are naturally fine.

When it comes to health, no human being gets to live in perfect conditions. The pressures of life, the food that we eat, the air that we breathe, the water that we drink, all these can affect us in many ways. The more our activities are in the world, the more we are exposed to many things that can throw our chemistry off balance and create health problems. But if the energy in our system is properly cultivated and kept active, these things will not have an effect. The physical body and the mental body will be in perfect health; there is no question about it.

See, life functions in many ways. Let us say you don't know anything about electricity. You do not know what electricity is. This hall is dark.

If I tell you to just press this button and the whole hall will be flooded with light, will you believe me? No. Now I just do it, and light appears. You will call it a miracle, isn't it? Simply because you don't understand how electricity works. Similarly, life happens in many different ways. But you have limited yourself to just the physical, the logical — physical in experience, logical in thinking.

Right now, medical sciences are limited to just knowing the physical body. If anything happens beyond that, you think it's a miracle. I just call it another kind of science, that's all. It is another kind of science. This life energy in you created your whole body — these bones, this flesh, this heart, these kidneys and everything. Do you think it cannot create health? If your energies are kept in full flow and proper balance, it is capable of much more than just health.

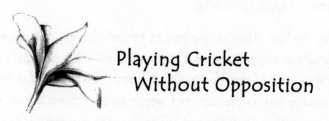

Playing Cricket
Without Opposition

Accepting the other team is most important.
When acceptance is total, there is no more opposition.

As children, we played a game simply because we enjoyed it. Slowly, sport has evolved into an investment opportunity. Take the Cricket World Cup for example. Sadly, as the players become more and more involved in the Championship, they forget the play. In fact, play becomes work. Only when players enjoy playing, they can perform their best.

Playing for India means fulfilling a billion people's expectations and that is not easy. When players start playing to satisfy other people's expectations, their minds are stressed and their physical activity also becomes limited.

When a man is truly happy and carefree, he can engage in incredible physical action. This is the main aspect of yoga for sport, that action can be performed without prior thought. With thought, intentions can be visible.

So one does not think, one simply acts, as is needed in this moment. When the players practise intensely, everything that they have to do on the field becomes like their second nature.

Action can simply flow out of them – as the game demands. This way, they can respond with agility to whatever the other team throws at them. With proper practice of yoga, bringing sufficient control over their mind and body, they can learn to act without prior thinking.

Playing Cricket Without Opposition

Meditation means going back to one's original nature. When one is simply with this breath, all identifications dissolve. It is impossible to meditate as a champion. Similarly, when playing a game, the cricketer should drop all identity.

If the cricketer constantly thinks of himself as per his identity, it would be very burdensome. Once he becomes 100% free of identity, he doesn't have to play the game. It just happens.

How is a cricketing legend born? Surely not because the team he played against was not competent. For such a player, coordination is at its peak. He knows what he wants in his life. He is so committed to what he wants, that it becomes a reality. If our cricketers can organise their energies, bodies and minds in such a way that they get more and more focused, everything happens for the best.

Cricket is just one form of activity the player has chosen. It is important that this person becomes truly aware – physically, mentally, emotionally and spiritually. Then whatever game he plays, he will play very well. When fools are playing cricket, cricket will be a foolish game. When intelligent people play cricket, it will be an intelligent game. It all depends on who is playing the game.

What the players make of themselves is more important than cricket. Without bringing a certain quality into themselves, they cannot bring quality into the game. If they cultivate humility, they can aspire to reach unimaginable heights of performance. Humility is just acceptance of what is. Out of this acceptance, they can use their intelligence and act.

Acceptance is important to connect to a situation and to respond to the situation intelligently. Accepting the other team is most important. When acceptance is total, there is no more opposition.

Only if the other eleven people are there can a game be played – only then is a match possible. With acceptance, there is no tension. The other team's capabilities and victory record will no more be a problem. With total acceptance, their presence will diminish. This is a spiritual process also. When acceptance is total, the entire existence becomes a part of oneself. This is the way of nature.

Rat Race Winner
– Still A Rat!

You want to race with everybody because you want to be one up on everybody, especially your neighbor. But you do not want to face the difficulties that arise due to this competition.

If you leave out compassion, what is left? You can only be an animal. Society is in that state right now. If you survey the challenges of today's world, one can easily come to a dismaying conclusion. There is great competition. Those who want to compete can compete. If you don't need the race, why don't you come out? Or at least why can't you slow down the pace? No, you want to race with everybody because you want to be one up on everybody, especially your neighbor. But you do not want to face the difficulties that arise due to this competition. You should understand this very clearly — whatever action you perform in your life, there is a consequence to it. There is no such thing as you must perform only this type of action and you must not perform another type of action. You can do anything. But you must be in a state to accept the consequences joyously.

After performing the action, crying when you have to face the consequences will not do. Do whatever you want in your life, but tomorrow, when you have to face the consequences, you should not cry and complain. If you can accept this joyously, you can do anything. If you don't have the energy to accept the consequence, you don't have to perform that action! It is not needed. Just because somebody else is doing something, you don't have to attempt it or do it. You do not know the kind of energy they have. Isn't it? So, the society has not only become competitive; you are caught in the rat race. You can compete to the extent you want to. But if you don't have the need for competition, then come, we will teach you meditation; we will set you on the path of meditation – not because you are useless for anything else, only because the need to compete, the need to be in the rat race has dropped.

Standing By To Understand

The closer the relationship is, the more effort you should make to understand them.

Standing By To Understand

When you live in this world, there are various types of complex interactions happening. As your field of play increases, the complexity of interaction also increases. If you're just sitting in a cubicle, working on your computer with only one other person, you need only a little understanding, but if you're managing a thousand people, you need a vast understanding of everybody. Now, suppose you're managing a thousand people and you want all these people to understand you, then you're not going to manage anything. You need to understand the limitations and the capabilities of these thousand people and do what you can; only then will you have the power to move the situation the way you want it to go. If you're waiting for these thousand people to understand you and act, it is only a pipe dream; it is never going to happen.

The closer the relationship is, the more effort you should make to understand them. Somebody becomes closer and dearer to you only as you understand him better. If they understand you, they enjoy the closeness of the relationship. If you understand them better, then you enjoy the closeness. It is not that the other person is totally bereft of understanding. With your understanding you can create situations where the other person would be able to understand you better. If you're expecting the other one to understand and comply with you all the time while you don't understand the limitations, the possibilities, the needs and the capabilities of that person, then conflict is all that will happen;

it is bound to happen. Unfortunately, the closest relationships in the world have more conflict going on than between enemies.

In your relationships, you have fought many more battles than this and are still fighting; isn't it so? This is because your line of understanding and theirs is different. If you cross this L.O.C., this Line of Control, they will get mad. If they cross it, you will get mad. If you move your understanding beyond theirs, their understanding also becomes a part of your understanding. You will be able to embrace their limitations and capabilities. In everyone, there are some positive aspects and some negative aspects. If you embrace all this in your understanding, you can make the relationship the way you want it. If you leave it to their understanding, it will become accidental. If they are very magnanimous, things will happen well for you; if not, the relationship will break up.

All I am asking is: do you want to be the one who decides what happens to your life? Whether they are intimate relationships, professional, political, global or whatever, don't you want to be the person who decides what happens in your life? If you do, you better include everything and everybody into your understanding. You should enhance your understanding to such a point that you can look beyond people's madness also. There are very wonderful people around you, but once in a while they like to go crazy for a few minutes. If you don't understand that, you will lose them. If you don't understand their madness, you will definitely lose them. If you do, then you know how to handle them. Life is not always a straight line; you have to do many things to keep it going. If you forsake your understanding, your capability will be lost. Whether it's a question of personal relationships or professional management, in both places you need understanding; otherwise, you won't have fruitful relationships.

The way you are right now, the very quality of your life is decided by the type of relationships you hold. You better make the needed effort to understand the people around you.

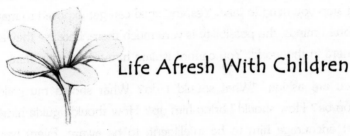

Life Afresh With Children

*Your child should do something that you did not even
dare to think of in your life.*

The first thing to do when bringing up a child is not to touch your children, not to influence their minds with your distorted minds. That is the first step you need to take. Yes, the child can get exposed to many other rotten minds, the possibility is very much there, because they are everywhere in the world. You cannot isolate him totally from that.

Now you are asking: "What should I do? What should my child's education be? How should I bring him up? How should I guide him?" You just encourage him to be intelligent, to be aware. Every being has been given the necessary intelligence to fulfill his life. An ant is born, you study it and see. It has all the intelligence to live an ant's life fully. It may not be able to do what you are doing, but as an ant, the necessary intelligence for being an ant is there for it. The same goes for every creature. You too have the necessary intelligence to live your life to the fullest.

Now, the problem is that you want your child to be intelligent your way, not his. Your idea of intelligence is that your child should become a doctor. Maybe he would have made a wonderful carpenter, but you want him to become a doctor. Not because doctors are needed in the world, not because you care so much to relieve the suffering that you want your child to dedicate himself as a doctor, but simply because you have a stupid idea in your head that in the social structure, a doctor or an engineer means some kind of prestige or some nonsense for you: "My child is a doctor!" You want to live your life through your children. This is a sure way to destroy children. This is a definite way to destroy children.

Your child need not do what you did in life. Your child should do something that you did not even dare to think of in your life. You did not have the courage to even nurture a thought like that – your child should do that – only then this world will progress and something will happen, isn't it?

Every child does have the necessary intelligence to live his life fully. You just create an atmosphere for him to grow into his intelligence, rather than imposing your nonsense upon him. When it comes to influencing him, the teachers will have a role, his friends, other sections of the society will have some influence on him. You can't help it; you cannot build a sanatorium for your child, but still, as a parent, you can play a very important role in allowing the child's intelligence to bloom.

First of all, if you have come to the idea that when a child is born, it is time to teach, then you will ruin the child. When a child comes into your life, it is a time to learn, because you have missed much in your life and so much of you has become distorted. Now, a child is just looking at life. You sit with him and look at life afresh. The only thing that you can do to your child is to give him love and support; his intelligence will grow. That is all. Create a loving atmosphere for him where intelligence will naturally flower.

Life Afresh With Children

People understand that to bring up a child lovingly means to get him everything that he asks for. If you look at your child with intelligence, do you see that getting him everything that he asks for is sheer stupidity? To this, you have given the name "love". So how should you bring up a child? In whichever situation he is put, he should be able to live joyously, isn't it? That is the way he should be brought up.

If you want to bring up your child well, the first thing is that you should be happy. Right now, you, by yourself, do not know how to be happy. Everyday in your house, there is a demonstration of tension, anger, fear, anxiety and jealousy. Only these things are being demonstrated to your child. What will happen to him? He will learn only this. If you really have the intention of bringing up your child well, you must first change your way of being. If you are incapable of transforming yourself, where is the question of you bringing up your child?

What's The Big Deal
That You Are Upto Today?

You have become a disciple of the devil if your whole life is about making deals. The devil is always making a deal with somebody.

What's The Big Deal That You Are Upto Today?

If you really want the best deals in life, don't try to make deals. You must be in such a way that your client should, as a businessman or a trader, fall in love with you in every way. This is not a trick. The deal will happen if it's necessary; it won't happen if it's not. The deal is for both people's well-being, so it must be needed by both of you. Once we live in the world, there are transactions. Some are of a personal nature, others are different. All of them affect your life.

What is it that you call a love affair? It is unconditional involvement and doing whatever is needed. If you don't have that sense of involvement, you will always try to get the best deal out of somebody. That means you must meet the dumbest people in the world. Intelligent people will never bite your dumb deals. If you just give yourself and see how both of you can be benefited from the deal, then whenever it is possible, it will happen. Of course, deals are subject to many other conditions such as market situations, economic conditions or the world situation, but if you establish your inner way of being and are doing the best you can do, then what has to happen, according to your capability, will happen. What you can't do won't happen anyway. Even if you break your head it won't happen, but that's okay.

You have become a disciple of the devil if your whole life is about making deals. The devil is always making a deal with somebody. God never made a deal with anybody. Maybe you haven't attained to your full Divine nature, but in this case at least let us imitate God for a while. God doesn't make deals. Deals will be offered to you in so many ways. In a way, everybody is just a businessman. Everybody is trying to pull off some deal: some in the market place, another maybe at home, another maybe in the temple, and a few maybe even with their spiritual process, but everybody is trying to pull off some kind of a deal. When you get a good deal, you are all very civilized and nice but if a deal goes bad, you will yell and scream.

You need not be a super human being capable of doing everything. If you don't do what you're capable of doing, that's when it's not okay; that's when you have failed. So don't worry about always pulling off deals, deals and more deals. Just learn to offer yourself, which is the best possible thing that you can offer to the whole situation. Then naturally people will take it if it's what they need.

Whether you talk to a taxi driver for a minute, or you talk to your boss, or speak to your client, husband, wife or child, every transaction is affecting your life. Now the problem with you is that you hold one transaction above the other. You involve yourself more with one and less with the other. It won't work like that. All these things are needed for you to have a fruitful life. Why don't you just fall in love with the whole situation? As long as you wish to be in that situation, make it happen like a huge love affair. Why not? That's how it should be. Only then work becomes effortless.

Act In The Context Of Action

*Right now, why you think in terms of right and wrong is
simply because of the social moral code.*

The nature of karma is not in the action that you perform. Karma means action, but this gathering of past karmas is not because of the actions you have performed. It is the volition, the intention, the kind of mind that you carry. That is your karma.

There is a story that Ramakrishna used to tell. There were two friends who used to go visit a prostitute every Saturday evening. On one such evening, while they were walking towards the prostitute's house, there was someone giving a spiritual discourse. One friend decided not to visit the prostitute, saying he would prefer to hear the lecture on spiritual possibilities. The other man left him there. Now the man sitting in the lecture hall, his thoughts were full of the other man. He began thinking that the other man was having the time of his life while he himself was caught in this place. He thought the other man was more intelligent in choosing the prostitute's place rather than a spiritual discourse.

Now the man who had gone to the prostitute's house, his mind was full of the other man. He began to think that his friend had chosen the path to liberation by preferring the spiritual discourse to the prostitute's place, while he got caught in this. The man who had gone for the spiritual discourse and was thinking about what was happening in the prostitute's house pays by piling up bad karma. He suffers, not the other man. You don't pay because you have gone to the prostitute;

you pay because you are cunning about it. You still want to go there, but you think by going to the discourse you'll be one step closer to heaven. This cunningness will take you to hell. That man with the prostitute knows it is worthless, and seeks something else; his is good karma. So it is not about action.

Right now, why you think in terms of right and wrong is simply because of the social moral code. It is not your innate nature which is telling you that this is right and wrong. It is just that society has fixed some rules and they have always told you, right from your childhood, that if you break them, you are a bad boy. So whenever you break these, you feel like a bad boy. If you feel like one, you become one. If you are used to gambling, maybe gambling in front of your mother or your wife, in your home, or even to utter the word is sacrilege, but once you join your gang, there gambling is just fine, isn't it?

Among the gamblers, the one who does not gamble is not fit to live. It's like this everywhere. If all of you are thieves, you are all fine, isn't it? Among thieves, do they feel it is bad to rob somebody? When you fail, they think you are a no-good thief. That is a bad karma, isn't it? The question, this karmic thing, is just the way you feel about it. It is not about what you are doing. It is just the way you are holding it in your mind. Why we are talking about acceptance, acceptance, acceptance, is, if you are absolute acceptance, whatever life demands, you do. If you have to fight a battle, you go and fight, there is no karma. The karma is not made in physical action; it is made only by volition. It's just that some fool has formed some rules and you expect every human being to live by them. It's impossible, but society needs such rules to maintain the social ego.

The society has its own ego, isn't it? For every small thing, the whole society gets upset. It need not be wrong. Suppose it is summer in the United States. Everybody is hardly wearing anything or maybe they are in miniskirts. Let's say you are fully clothed. People will get upset: "What is she doing? Why is she all covered up?" Here in India, if you don't dress like that, they will all get upset! So this is one kind of ego; that is another kind of ego. It is the social ego which is getting upset, and your karma is becoming part of the collective karma. I want you to really understand this with a certain depth. Your idea of good and bad has been taught to you. You have imbibed it from the social atmosphere in which you have lived. Karma is in the context of your life, and not in the action itself.

 ## Saturday Night Fever

*Today, it has become a common phenomenon in society
that everybody is in some level of neurosis. This is simply
because your energy is not worked out; it's trapped.*

The whole world is going through a unique kind of neurosis, which was not there in the past. This is simply because modern man has stopped using his body to a large extent. In the past, when you intensely involved yourself in physical activity, a lot of your neurosis was worked out. Your nervous energy got spent. I know many people, especially young people, who had psychological problems. They just started swimming or playing some sport daily and then everything became okay; because of enough activity, the energy was expended.

Today, man has become physically inactive like never before – he could not afford to be so physically inactive before, he had to do so many things physically, just to survive. He has become more neurotic than in the past. As a general phenomenon, there were neurotic people then also, but not in these numbers. Today, it has become a common phenomenon in society that everybody is in some level of neurosis. This is simply because your energy is not worked out; it's trapped. You have not transcended your madness and at the same time you're not working it out. The therapy also is not there. If you went out and chopped wood for the whole day – if you chopped a hundred logs a day – a lot of your energy would be spent, and life would be peaceful; but today it's not like that. You are not using your body the way it used to be used, so you go on generating all kinds of diseases, like never before.

Saturday Night Fever

This builds up into your system over a period of time. Then your physical and emotional energy needs some outlet. That is how your bars, your clubs and your discotheques have come into place. People have to work out their neurosis somewhere, somehow. These discos look like madness, you can't even breathe inside. They are full of smoke and sweat but people are just going wild. You can't even dance, everybody is bumping into everybody else, but it doesn't matter, you have to work it out, otherwise you will go crazy. So on Saturday, you go work out your neurosis for the week. Then the piling up starts once more and once again the Saturday night fever comes.

There is another way to drop this madness and go ahead. Completely leaving it behind and going ahead where you are no more a part of it. This is what meditation is all about. Now, if you dance, you simply dance for the joy of it, and not because there is something to work out. If you're dancing to work out something, maybe it is therapeutic. It is good therapy, alright, but there is a certain ugliness about it. It is lusty; you cannot dance out of love. You can only dance out of lust.

Do you know the difference between love and lust? Lust is a strong need, love is not a need. When you love, you settle down, nothing more is needed. You can just sit here for a lifetime. With lust you can't sit anywhere, you either get into some mad action, or you are bound to go crazy. When there is a certain neurosis, a certain madness within yourself, you can only be in lust. Your lust can be for sex, for food or for some particular activity or some hobby, it doesn't matter what it is, but you develop lust for something. Without that lust you cannot live. Even your work is an effective way of throwing out your lust. It's just that it is the most popular and accepted way in the world. Today people just go on working, working and working. Not because they are creating something fantastic, but simply because they have to work, otherwise they don't know what to do with themselves.

You have to guard that madness cautiously. Nobody ever knows that you have this within yourself and you yourself would like to forget it. You do everything possible to forget it. All the entertainment in the world has come just to hide your madness. If you were perfectly sane, you would not need entertainment. You need entertainment just to cover your madness. If we take away your entertainment, you will go crazy. Man needs entertainment simply to hide his madness. If he was perfectly sane, he would not need entertainment. He could just sit and watch the bamboo grow. He would not really need entertainment.

Need Hundreds Of
Jesuses & Buddhas

Right now, religion is mostly about belonging to groups;
that's all it is doing to people.

Religion is an inward step, but if it is only about belonging to this group or that group, it is very unfortunate. That has only brought hatred, conflict and separation among people. The same people who are together today, the moment they identify with their religions, suddenly they separate. Tomorrow they are burning each other's homes. Ten minutes ago, they did not even think about such a thing. The moment they get identified to some religious group, they are willing to fight. If they did not belong to these groups, at least they would have no reason to fight. Maybe individuals would fight; but the whole group of people, they would have no reason to fight. Some individuals will fight for some personal reasons, that is different. But this kind of mass stimulation of animal energy wouldn't happen.

Right now, religion is mostly about belonging to groups; that's all it is doing to people. Religion should have made them Divine, but it is not even making them human. They are becoming like animals, because the moment you belong to a group, you want to protect your group. That is a natural reaction in you. It is a very basic human instinct. Once you are identified with a particular group, you are always a threat to another group. The moment you identify yourself with any one particular group, you become an enemy to the others. Maybe you'll talk to each other, you will be okay with each other, but the moment the lines are crossed, it is war.

Need Hundreds Of Jesuses & Buddhas

Definitely every individual truly wants peace, nobody wants conflict. But the moment he joins a group, he fights, isn't it? Individually, if you talk to them, nobody wants this nonsense. Bu the moment they are with a group, they lose their individual intelligence and are fired up with a different kind of emotion.

So why can't we talk about peace? It is time we talk about it. It is the new millennium, isn't it? Only if we start talking about it today, at least by the next millennium, some transformation in this situation may happen. If you don't dare talk about it, you will just push the world in this direction forever. The only reason why they crucified Jesus is because he dared to talk about it.

Once again the same things are happening with people. So this is not as if once you correct it, it will always remain corrected. No. It needs constant correction, all the time. Just one Jesus will not do; one Buddha will not do. Many are needed. Only then there is a possibility of keeping the world in some state of sanity. Otherwise, people will continue to go to the extremes.

Divine Choice:
To Rule Or To Serve

Normally, everybody wants to rule the world.

Divine Choice: To Rule Or To Serve

Creating what one wants generally has meant visualizing, imagining, dreaming, craving, longing, praying and begging. There is another way to create without asking for anything, without ever thinking about anything, where things just happen. Before we arrive at that, a little bit of fired-up movement is needed. People who have never been on fire will not know the coolness of water. People who have just lived their life in a halfhearted manner, sedately, can never know the other way. Becoming a fanatic at least for a while can be useful for your energies to reach a boiling point and get moving. Then, to transform them into something else is very easy. That is the whole purpose of karma or action.

Why a sadhaka[1] chooses action is just for this reason. We are going to perform action anyway. Now we have the choice whether we want to perform Hitler's or Mahatma Gandhi's type of action. Whichever way we feel is best right now, we do that. That's all there is to it. Anyway we have to perform action, so let us do it wholeheartedly, and let us choose the form of action that we want to do.

Do you know the self-image that you want? Do you want to rule the world or do you want to serve the world? Ultimately, that is the choice. Normally, everybody wants to rule the world. It is just that, because a man is halfhearted, he is only able to rule his wife. He does not get

---

1 *sadhaka*: spiritual seeker who undertakes yogic practices, usually under the guidance of a Master

to rule the world, so all he is able to do is rule his children, wife or something like that, but what he really wants is to rule the world. The fool doesn't have the capacity or the intensity to do it; otherwise, he would be a potential Hitler. The man who physically abuses his child or wife because they don't conform to his ideas, if tomorrow he is made the king of the world, will use a sword instead of a stick. That's all. It is just that he is incapable and doesn't have the intensity to rule the world; otherwise, he is already the ruler.

Now the choice is just this – either to rule or to serve. Whichever kind of image you think is most harmonious, the closest to Divinity and closest to realization, that kind of action you choose. Every moment, do it with tremendous intensity, without giving it a single moment's break. Then a day will come when action is not needed anymore. A man who does not know action – real action, intense action – can never move into inaction. If you try to, inaction will just become lethargy. Only if you have known intense action can you know inaction. People who are always resting in their life must be experts about rest, isn't it? But that is not the truth. Only a man who works intensely can know what rest is. So this non–doing business, if you really want to know it, first you must discover what doing is. You have not done that yet. In every waking moment of my life, unceasingly I pursue this work of offering myself, physically and mentally. Unceasingly I pursue it twenty–four hours of the day, every waking moment and even in my sleep, with tremendous intensity. It is only out of that, that all of this has happened in my life. It has become so powerful simply because it does not mean anything to me, but for twenty–four hours, I am at it. Now this has a different kind of power. That is the whole meaning of sacrifice. It is only out of that, that something else happens — both inside and outside — which can never be put into words.

Victims Of Crime

Unfortunately, for most people, fear, anger, hatred are the most intense situations in their lives. Their love is never so intense, their peace is never so intense, their joy is never so intense, but their negativities are intense.

Victims Of Crime

Usually, you are looking only at that person who is abused as a victim, but the person who is abusing is also a victim, because in many ways he is degrading himself. The worst thing that any human being can do to himself is to degrade himself like an animal, which for some reason he is doing. Though it may give him some pleasure or joy or power or something at that moment, still, in many ways, it is a tragedy for him as well. So it is not that one is a victim and the other an assailant. Both are victims. Many things like this are happening in the society; it is not just an individual act; it is a complex process of many things that are happening. So should you allow it to happen? No, you do whatever you can do to see that these things don't happen.

But these things do happen in the world. So what you can do, you do, but you cannot change all of it. It does not matter what kind of a human being you become, even if you become a super-human being, you will never have absolute control over the external world. Whether it is your institution or your family or the world, you will never have total control over the external situation.

But you can have total control over the internal situation. This is always possible. Now, the external has gone out of control. For some reason, people are killing, people are raping, people are doing all kinds of ugly things in the world. Does it mean to say that you should allow the internal to also go out of control? If your external situations are going out of control, is it not very important that at least you keep your interiority in control?

Now that man has gone insane; he is into that kind of act. If you are also going insane with anger and hatred for that man, what is the difference? He raped, so you want to kill. What is the difference? That does not mean you should not do something about the situation. What you have to do, you do. But when you do it with anger and hatred, it is of no value — whatever you do.

Unfortunately, for most people, fear, anger, hatred, are the most intense situations in their lives. Their love is never so intense, their peace is never so intense, their joy is never so intense, but their negativities are intense. So they experience power in negative situations.

As you experience power in anger, the rapist experiences his lust as power. It is the most powerful situation that he experiences in his life, where he physically imposes himself on somebody else. He feels powerful. That is why he is going for it. And that is exactly the justification you are giving to be angry. It is not different. It is just that the acts are different. One is socially approved and another is not approved. That is all. Otherwise both these actions are coming from the same basis.

Now you think that you can change the world, or that you have the capacity to move yourself only with anger. Why? Why can't you move with love? Why can't you move with compassion? Why can't you move out of your intelligence as to what is needed around you? Okay, not even out of love; at least out of your intelligence you do what is needed for the society around you. The most beautiful things will happen when your actions spring from your intelligence and not from your anger.

How you respond depends on what kind of situation you are in, who you are, what your capabilities are, what means you have to do that sort of a thing. You cannot respond in the same way in every situation. If you have the power and the means to do something effectively, you can respond in one way. If you do not have the power and the means to respond at that moment, maybe your response is to keep quiet at that moment and see what can be done later. But this is not done in vengeance or revenge.

You don't want this to happen, either to the victim or to the assailant. Both are in some way being degraded in their life. One is doing it to himself, another is being subjected to that by somebody. You don't want this to happen to either of them, not just one. Only then you can say that you are functioning from your love. Otherwise you are functioning only from your identity as a woman or man, which will not create a healthy world. Since people always act from their identity of belonging to a certain group, or religion, or race, or country, or sex, all this misery has happened...

So how you respond depends on what means you have. All of us cannot respond in the same way to any given situation. It depends on what means we have in our hands at that moment. If you get into wild reactions out of your emotions, you will not bring any justice. You will not bring any well-being to the world. You will just counter one evil with another evil. That is not a solution. Only when you act without identifications, when you just function out of your intelligence, can there be a solution to this.

A World Of Worldly Affairs

It takes tremendous maturity to simply sit quietly, only doing things to the extent that it is needed.

People ask me, "To seek the Divine, should one withdraw from worldly affairs?" See, how can you withdraw from worldly affairs anyway? What are you calling as worldly affairs? Let us say, I am tending to this coconut tree; it is very much a worldly affair, isn't it? I am cooking my own food; is it not a worldly affair? So you have worldly affairs, otherwise how can you live?

The kind of worldly affairs you want to do is your individual choice. For example, everyone doesn't have to join politics. In society, someone is into politics, someone else is just a clerk in an office, somebody else is running a whole industry, and someone is just sweeping floors. All of them are doing worldly affairs. So you cannot really withdraw from worldly affairs.

It is just a choice of what kind of worldly affairs you want to do in your life and how much. And why shouldn't any person have this choice? Every person definitely has the choice. It is only those people who do not know what they are doing with themselves and are just doing what everybody else is doing that complain in this manner. They don't know what to do by themselves. They neither have the intelligence nor the awareness to live their life by choice.

Such people are always complaining about spiritual people, "Oh, these people are not being responsible. They are not into worldly affairs, they are just doing their own affairs." The man who is in his own house or in his office is also there just to take care of his own affairs. He is not interested in the well-being of the world. He actually doesn't know what his real affair is and has gotten himself into such a mess that he doesn't even know how to get out of it. Because he is unable to get out, he thinks that somebody who is able to manage his own affairs the way he wants to in his life, to the extent that he wants to, is on the wrong bus.

It happened like this. One day, a drunk somehow pulled himself onto a bus, stumbled around over the passengers, knocked over suitcases and briefcases, came and landed on a seat next to a prim and proper old lady – and fell over on her. The lady pushed him and said, "I hate to say this, but you are going straight to hell." The drunk suddenly sprang up and said, "I am on the wrong bus then," and ran to get off.

So, drunken people do not know who is on the wrong bus. If others manage their lives to the extent they want to, these people who have made their lives unmanageable, enslaved and entangled in situations around them, become very jealous. They will always complain. They will say that these people are just running away from the world. Right now, the way the world is going, if a lot of people become over industrious and continue to do too many things on this planet, it will not even last another ten years. Fortunately, fifty percent of the people are lazy. The other fifty percent who are too industrious, are busy destroying the world. Probably only one percent is really spiritual. Now, we want to make at least fifty percent of them spiritual in order to save the world.

People who are withdrawing from excessive activity are not causing any damage either to themselves, the society, the world, the environment, or the planet. It is only people who are engaged in activity in absolute unawareness who are truly destroying this world, isn't it? In total unawareness, not knowing what they are doing, simply imitating someone, they are doing more damaging activity than anyone else. They are the people who are causing tremendous damage to the planet and really threatening life on it. They are the people who are taking the whole of humanity toward global suicide. So right now, the most responsible thing you can do in the world is to withdraw from unconscious activity, but withdrawing from activity is not so simple. It takes tremendous maturity to simply sit quietly, only doing things to the extent that it is needed. This doesn't come because you are lazy or irresponsible; it comes because you are aware and conscious.

Flexing Out Of Bondages

The complexities that one encounters on the spiritual path are not because of the path. The complexities are only there because of the mess that is your mind.

During the practice of *yoga asanas*[1] you realize how rigid you are physically. It takes a little more awareness for you to know the rigidity in your mind and emotions. Somebody who is very rigid in his thoughts and emotions believes that he is perfect because he does not allow room for any other way of looking, thinking or feeling. When you meet this man, you think he is pig–headed, but he thinks he is perfect. Similarly, there can be rigidity on the energy level. For someone whose energy is very fluid, on the very first day of the simplest *yoga kriya*[2], the energy will start moving and transforming, whereas for another person, even after practicing it for a long time, nothing seems to happen. This simply depends on how malleable the energies are. The rigidity in all these dimensions isn't really separate, they are all interconnected. The rigidity in one dimension manifests itself into the others.

On Patanjali's path, yoga is a system where it doesn't matter what kind of a fool you are, what level of unawareness you're in, what kind of karmic bondages you have; there is still a way for you. If you are willing to at least bend your body, you have already broken one karma. If your forehead touches your knee, then you have broken a physical karma. This is not a joke; it's quite an achievement for a person who has never done it before. This simple limitation would have increased with the passage of time. Even the little flexibility that's there in you

---

1 *asana*: lit. seat; generally referring to yogic postures; one of the eight limbs of yoga

2 *kriya*: lit. action; certain yogic practices to transform one's energies

today will become less as time goes by. A day will come when you're totally rigid, both physically and mentally.

This is happening to everybody. Look at your own life; see how flexible you were at the age of ten or twelve, both physically and mentally. At the age of twenty, the flexibility is considerably less and at the age of thirty, most of it is gone. Not only physically, mental rigidity has also set in very severely as you progress on this path; it's not progression, rather it is regression. Life is just a regression for most people. They are not growing; they are going backwards. Even with what little assets they have come, they don't grow; they just go backwards, unfortunately. Whatever advantage you were born with, you haven't enhanced it; you have only taken it backwards.

The path is actually very simple, but because of your personality it has become extremely complicated. The path by itself is not complicated. The complexities that one encounters on the spiritual path are not because of the path. The complexities are only there because of the mess that is your mind. Nothing moves within you. You become rigid, as if rigor mortis has set in. You need the Master's Grace to quell the madness of your mind.

If you allow the Master's Grace, then the path is very simple, as the path is the destination. If you simply sit here now, your whole being will pulsate with the existence.

You have kept your energies suppressed to such an extent, the mind has become so oppressive that it suppresses life to the point where nothing moves except what is needed to support the ego. Your energies are moving only to the extent that is convenient for your ego; a little more energy and the ego will burst. The moment energy rises within you, everything is dissolved. The ego knows it very well. That is why it has kept it suppressed. If you don't have any energy, then again the ego will become very weak. When all energy is cut off, the ego will feel very weak and it doesn't like that.

So it just allows the amount of energy which supports and feeds it well. If the energy becomes too much, the ego will be shattered. If kundalini[1] begins to rise, everything will be shattered and nothing will be left. You will be just a force merging with everything around you. You won't have a will of your own anymore. Since you are not willing to surrender your will, we are prodding you through this sadhana[2] to provoke your energies. That is why the path of asana and kriya. Since you are not able to do it by yourself, just activate creation itself in a certain way. If it begins to move, it settles everything. It is like a flood; your centuries-old world is wiped away in only a few hours of fury. So your sadhana is not about getting somewhere. It is just a way, a method to unleash a flood so enormous that it wipes away your petty creations and leaves you as the Creator intended you to be.

1 *kundalini*: lit. serpent power; life energy which is depicted as a snake coiled at the base of the spine (muladhara chakra) and that eventually, through the practice of yoga, rises upto sahasrar chakra.

2 *sadhana*: spiritual practices

Flowers On The Path

Good & Bad
Divide The World

The moment you say something is bad, you can't stop disliking it, can you?

People always believe that they are good and somebody else is bad. That's the only way they can carry on their missions in the world. Right now, we're on this part of the Himalayan road; they are making it into a two-lane highway. Every year, so many people die here because of landslides and vehicles going off the road. Driving these curves, one mistake and you've had it. When you travel here, you give an enormous responsibility to the driver. Just one mistake of his and you're finished. Every year, so many people make those mistakes. If you don't know this, when you see a small heap of scrap metal on the side of the road, it's usually a salvaged vehicle.

So they are laying a two-lane highway. Is it good or bad? People like you can travel in more comfort, with less risk, so that's good. Today, a lot of people may tell you to stop building roads, disfiguring the mountain, and disturbing the creatures on this planet. So for them, this is bad. Just because those in power, or the majority, think something is good, it won't become good. Maybe it would be better to take a person as an example. Now whatever a terrorist is doing, is it good or bad?

You may say bad. In the same situation, who is good and who is bad all depends on which side of the border you're on. Is India good or is Pakistan good? You're on this side of the border, so obviously Indians are good; Pakistanis are evil. If you were on the other side of the border, you would be arguing for the other side. It all depends on what you're identified with. Accordingly, you have your "goods" and "bads". You cannot think beyond that.

Your thinking itself is limited to your identifications. Your identifications are always limited, so your thinking is also limited. With this limitedness, why do you get into this nonsense about deciding what's good or bad? The moment you say something is bad, you can't stop disliking it, can you? Can you say, "This is a bad person, but that's okay with me"? On the surface you may say it, but if he gets closer to you, though initially it is just dislike, later it will turn to hate. The moment you identify something as good or bad, you're just dividing the world.

Now somebody comes and says they want to walk the spiritual path. So I tell them, "Okay, stay here for a week. Let us see what we can do." Then he says, "No, no, Saturday is my cousin's birthday; I have to go. I can be here only for three days." So I ask, "All right, but how far would you like to go with this?" He says, "All the way." Then I say, "So in three days, all the way? Anyway, you do these few things when you're here, then let's see what to do next." Then he says, "No, I don't like this." So I tell him, "Okay, you give me a list of things that you like. We will do only that." He sits there, thinks seriously for a while and writes down half a dozen things. So I ask, "What? In this vast existence, you like just about half a dozen things, and with that, you want to be spiritual?" Where is the possibility?

The moment you create good and bad, you are dividing the world. Once you divide it, where is the question of inclusion? Where is the question of yoga? Where is the question of becoming one with everything? Where is the question of knowing truth? Your division is because of your stupidity; it has got nothing to do with reality. Good and bad are always according to your ego requirements. If you go by this, you enslave yourself to the dualities of life; you divide the existence. So the question of turning spiritual never arises.

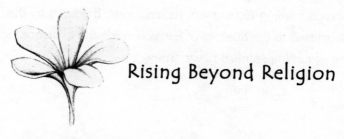

Rising Beyond Religion

You believe in things that you have not seen and experienced. This has become the basis of all conflict.

The moment man became religious should have been the end of all conflict, but unfortunately, everywhere in the world, religion has become the main source of conflict. This has taken the maximum number of lives and caused the maximum amount of pain on the planet for thousands of years. This is only because people believe in something that is not a reality for them. Somebody believes in something, somebody else believes in something else, and naturally conflict cannot be avoided. Today or tomorrow they are going to fight. They may avoid conflict for some time, but some day they will fight. As long as you believe that only your way is right, and somebody else believes his way is right, you are bound to fight.

Though all religions started as an inward path, over time they have gotten twisted up and have simply become a set of beliefs. Though all religions have taught about the value of a human life, for the sake of the same religion, today you are willing to take each other's lives. Unfortunately, much pain and conflict has risen in this planet because of this. This basic problem has not been properly addressed. People are always trying to do patch up jobs between one group and the other, but they do not last for long and somewhere conflict will arise – the basis being, people only believe in something, something which is not yet a reality for them. If you come down to reality, it is the same reality for everybody, no matter what religious background you come from. When you come to belief, each group has their own belief of what is right and what is wrong, what is true and what is false. You believe in things that you have not seen and experienced. This has become the basis of all conflict.

The basic purpose of yoga has always been to pursue religion as an experience, as an inner experience, not as a belief. Don't start with any belief; start looking inward. Whatever is true, experience it and go further, approach it as a science, not as a belief. In yoga, we just see that fundamentally a human being can grow or reach his Ultimate Nature, God or the Divine, or whatever you would like to call it, by approaching it either through the body, the mind, emotion, or through inner energies. These are the only four realities that you know. Everything else is imagined. Everything else has been taught to you.

These are the four basic ways of yoga. If the body is used for growth, it is *karma yoga*. If the mind or intelligence is used, it is *gnana yoga*. If emotion – love and devotion are used, then it is *bhakti yoga*. If you transform your energies and grow, it is *kriya yoga*. This is just like referring to head, heart, hands and energy. That is what you are; that is what every human being is. Nobody is all head, or all heart, or all hands, or all energy, they are a combination of these four dimensions.

So, if a person has to grow, he needs a combination of these four paths of bhakti, gnana, kriya and karma. All the four need to be there in your life, only then there is growth. Only then there is a possibility of reaching the Ultimate Nature. Otherwise we have groups, and groups, and groups — quarrelling groups everywhere. Spiritually, there is nothing happening. Unless something of true value happens within a person, nothing of tremendous value can be done in the external world. Whatever you do, it is only your quality that you are going to spread. Whether you like it or not, this is the reality. Who you are is what you are going to spread everywhere. If you are concerned about the world, the first thing is that you must be willing to transform yourself.

Yoga is about "I am willing to change myself." This is not about wanting to change the world — you are willing to change. Only when you are willing to change, a change can really happen in this world. But when you say, "I want everybody else to change," only conflict will occur. Only when you are willing to change, there will be transformation. It is this self-transformation that will lead to true well-being for the individual and the society. This is a true revolution.

Bursting The Bubble Of Life

What you call a person is just like a bubble. This bubble doesn't have any substance of its own.

If you look up in the sky during the day, you see the sun. That becomes most dominant in your experience. In the night, if you look up, the stars become very dominant in your experience, but both the sun and the stars — and sun also happens to be a star — are very puny little things when compared to the vastness of the sky. Generally though, that is never in your perception. So, true existence is the vastness of the sky. The sun, the stars, you and me, are just small happenings, brief happenings really.

Today, modern science is telling you that even the sun has a life span. It is going to burn itself out. As you are burning your life out, similarly, the sun is on fever and it is burning its life out too. Your normal temperature is ninety-eight point six degrees Fahrenheit or whatever; the sun's normal temperature is some ninety-eight million degrees, but it also has a life span. It is also burning up. One day it will do itself in. So whatever you see as physical existence is just a small happening. The true existence is the vastness, the emptiness that is there, the space.

What you call a person is just like a bubble. This bubble doesn't have any substance of its own. The air was there. It just created a shell around it, so suddenly it has a different quality of its own. There are thick bubbles, there are thin bubbles, there are strong bubbles, there are weak bubbles, there are big bubbles, and there are small bubbles

– just like people. Just like every other creature too, but when the bubble bursts, the substance that is inside the bubble, where is it? The air has reclaimed it; the atmosphere has reclaimed it. Similarly, a bubble is formed in the form of an etheric body, in the form of a pranic body, a mental body and a physical body. The physical body we can shoot down any moment we want to. It is within our power to just cut the physical body in two if we want to, but the other bodies we are not able to cut. Only what you call as existence, only that can do it.

What you are calling the spiritual process is just that. It is a deeper way of suicide. This is not about killing the physical body. You are trying to destroy the very fundamentals of creating the body within you. You are trying to destroy the very fundamental structure over which a body can form. The physical body is possible only because of the necessary karmic substances that are there in the form of etheric, pranic and mental bodies.

So you are trying to destroy that through the spiritual process. With your awareness, with your practices, with your love, with your devotion, all you are trying to do is destroy the possibility of taking on another body, destroy the very foundation over which the physical body can happen. Or, in other words, we are trying to take away the possibility of you going through the recycling bin over and over again. A mother's womb is only a recycling bag. Again and again...going through the same process. So we want to take that away.

Why Are You Missing?

God is not somewhere, he is here and now.
It is you who is not.

Why Are You Missing?

If you fix the goal of your life, you will not miss anything. There are tendencies within everybody. The past karmas have influences over you, they push you this way and that way. All your passions, all your desires, you cannot fight with them. Don't ever try to fight with your passions and desires. Fighting with them is like fighting the demon, Mahishasura. If one drop of his blood falls, a thousand Mahishasuras will rise up. Your desires and passions are just like that. If you try and fight with them, if you chop them, they will spill blood, and with every drop, a hundred or a thousand will come up. There is no point fighting them. Just educate your passions, educate your desires to flow in the right direction, that is all.

Desire the highest in life. All your passions, direct them to the highest. Even if you get angry, direct it only toward the highest. Even with your passion, that is the way to do it. Right now, every bit of energy that you have, you expend it by making it into desire, passion, fear, anger, and many other things. Maybe these emotions are not in your hands for now, but channeling them in one direction is in your hands. Maybe when you are angry you cannot be loving, you cannot suddenly turn your anger into love, but the anger itself can be directed. Anger is tremendous energy, isn't it? Direct it in the right way, that is all. Every ounce of energy that you have, every passion, emotion, thought, if focused in one direction, the results can be very, very quick. Things will happen. Once you know there is something higher and you want to be there, there should be no other question about it.

Now, for you, again and again, this spirituality, this enlightenment, this God-realization looks so far away. It appears to be close this moment, the next moment it appears to be light years away, so certain complacency will come. They have always told you: "A bird in hand is worth two in the bush." What is there now is better than something somewhere else. What you need to understand is, it is not somewhere else, it is all here and now. Only because *you* are not, it looks like that for you. God is not somewhere, he is here and now. It is you who is not. That is the only problem. It is not difficult, but definitely it's not easy. It is extremely simple. Moving from here, from wherever you are right now, to the infinite is very simple, because it is right here. Do know, "simple" need not necessarily be easy. It is just subtle and delicate. Unless you put your whole life energy into it, it will not open up.

With halfhearted appeals, God never comes. With halfhearted appeals, realization never happens. It has to be everything; only then it can happen in one moment. It need not take twelve years. Probably a fool takes twelve years to become intense enough; that is different. If you make yourself intense enough, it is just one moment. After that, life is just blessed. You simply live on, whichever way you want, whatever way you choose. But without creating that one moment, going on doing all kinds of nonsense, what is the use?

Rushing Past The Past

*If every moment, one is like a snake leaving the skin behind,
only then there is growth.*

Right now, whatever you call as "yourself" is simply a certain formation of the mind you have collected. It is a certain type of information in your mind. When you say, "I'm a good person", "I'm a bad person", "I am haughty", "I am meek" or whatever you may say, all those things are simply certain formations of the mind, or in other words, it is just past accumulation. You simply live through your past. If the past is taken away, most people are just lost. Everything depends on the past. It is the previous moment which rules everything. This moment is not important. As long as the personality is important, it simply means the previous moment is important. This present moment is not important, because the personality belongs to the past.

In this moment you really have no personality, do understand this. The personality that you carry is a dead thing. When you're carrying a dead body over your shoulders, you can't walk very far. With a dead body, which way can you head? Only to the burial ground, isn't it? If you carry a dead body for too long, you will have to bear with terrible smells. Your personality, the stronger it is, the more odoriferous it is. You can go far in life only when you can leave your past. This is like a snake shedding its skin. Do you know how a snake sheds its skin? One moment it is a part of its body, the next moment it sheds its skin and just goes on without turning back. If every moment, one is like a snake leaving the skin behind, only then there is growth.

Rushing Past The Past

Only a person who does not carry the previous moment to this moment, only that person is free from everything, and that quality will be felt everywhere. Within a few moments of meeting you, people will trust you to the extent that they would not even trust their parents, or husbands, or wives, simply because you don't carry the burden of the past with you. If you carry the past with you, then you will also smell like anybody else. The whole world stinks with personalities. Everybody has his own strong smell or personality. These are the various stenches in the world, and they keep clashing all the time. When one does not carry this odor, one can cross over this existence. One not only passes through this world effortlessly, one will pass through the very process of life and death effortlessly. This person crosses the ocean of *samsara* [1] without any effort. What looks like a great effort for somebody else will be happening for this person without any effort. Everything just simply happens.

There may have been some moments in your life when you felt true compassion towards something or somebody. In those moments, all your personality, who you are, what you are, everything would have melted. Nothing would have been there. You are simply there in that moment.

---

1 *samsara*: world; the cycle of birth, death and rebirth

Mind: The Dumping Ground

*Only if you know to what extent your logic should go
and where it should not go, your life will be beautiful.*

Mind: The Dumping Ground

The more people think, the less joyful they are becoming in their lives. It should not be so.

Your mind is just society's garbage bin. Anybody who walks by you stuffs something in your head and goes. You really have no choice, whatever comes and hits any of the sense organs, either a vision or a sound or a sensation or a taste or a smell that touches your sense organs gets stored in the mind. So what you call as mind, the accumulative part of the mind is subject to the kind of social, religious and cultural situations you are being exposed to.

We could make the mind into three parts. The discriminatory dimension of the mind, which is called the intellect; the accumulative part that gathers information; and awareness, which is called *pragna*.

The very way you think, feel and understand life is just what kind of garbage you gathered in your head. Some of you have social garbage, religious garbage, spiritual garbage, it doesn't matter. But all this has come from outside. It's of survival significance only. It is not of any life significance. Your ability to recycle the garbage is your intellect. Your survival on this planet is possible only because you are able to discriminate between one thing and the other.

The more intellectual you become, the more you start splitting everything around you and it doesn't know where to stop. It doesn't allow you to be with anything totally. Intellect is a wonderful instrument for survival, at the same time intellect is a terrible barrier for you to experience the Oneness of life. Only if you know to what extent your logic should go and where it should not go, your life will be beautiful.

All the impressions that have entered your mind have entered you only through your five sense organs. And sense organs can perceive everything only in comparison. If you had not seen darkness in your life, you wouldn't know what is light.

Sense perception is giving you a distorted impression of reality because sense organs experience everything only in comparison with something else. And when there is a comparison there is always duality. You can only perceive in parts. So your perception is all in bits and pieces and these will never make the whole.

Now if you wipe it with awareness, this intellect can cut through what is true and what is not true. When your intellect becomes razor sharp, so that nothing sticks to it, it doesn't get attached to anything, it is not identified with anything, it just makes you see everything simply the way it is. It is not influenced by your accumulation, by your identifications, by your emotions.

The whole process of yoga and meditation is just this, once you have a clear space between you and your mind it is a completely different dimension of existence.

Limited Sense Of Sense Organs

If you are seeking something beyond survival, then the sense perceptions are not enough.

You have never experienced any power beyond yourself, except nature. Now, this wind that is blowing here, you are not blowing it, isn't it? This much is very clear to you. The wind blows with tremendous power; but you did not start this wind. And you did not create yourselves; you just happen to be here. Without that energy or that something which is beyond you, nothing can happen. Something must have created you.

Now that you do not know what created you, the next immediate thing you will say is that God must have done it. Now where has God come from? Since you are a human being, you think that God is a big human being. If you were a buffalo, you would think God is a big buffalo. So, whatever your idea of God is, it is simply coming from the limited experience of who you are right now. It is not coming from any true experience. It is only coming from a limited imagination. You are in human form, so you think God is one big human being. So, whatever you call as God, or power, you are only either thinking or imagining it. It is only in your mind. The only thing that you can really experience is that which is within you. And that which is within you, you have never really looked at in real depth.

Whatever you have known till now, your experience is only limited to your five sense organs. Whatever you have known, either of the world, or yourself, has come to you only by seeing, hearing, smelling, touching and tasting. If these five senses go to sleep, you will neither know the world nor yourself. The sense organs are limited perceptions. They feel everything only in comparison to something else. Now if I touch a steel rod, it feels cool to me simply because my body temperature is in a certain way. Suppose I lower my temperature and touch it, it will feel warm to me. So, this is not a genuine experience. This is an experience that is just sufficient to survive in the physical reality. Whatever experience you have through the five sense perceptions is a sufficient experience only for survival in this existence.

But if you are seeking something beyond survival, then the sense perceptions are not enough. So all yogic practices are fundamentally aimed at giving you an experience beyond the five sense perceptions. Whatever you experience beyond the five sense perceptions is not in terms of physical reality; it is in a different dimension. That dimension, if you want to call it God, call it God, or if you want to just call it power, power. Or if you want to call it my Self, call it my Self. You call it whichever way you like. Whatever name you give, it always gets misunderstood by people. The moment you give it a name, people misunderstand it in some way. Always. It does not matter what you call it. You call it "Shiva", "Allah", "God", or "Divine", but the moment you say it, within ten minutes misunderstandings will happen within people's minds.

So, right now the whole experience of transcending your limitations, can it come from within you, or does it happen from outside of you? That is the basic question. Now, if you want to transcend, only if you are truly willing it can happen, otherwise no power on earth or in heaven can move you.

 One Next Step At A Time

The whole process of yoga is to take you from something
that you know and take the next step into the unknown.

The word "yoga" literally means "union". When you experience everything as one in your consciousness, then you are in yoga. To attain to that unity within you there are many ways, for example: hatha yoga. Hatha yoga means you start with the body. The body itself has its own attitudes, its own ego, its own nature. Apart from your mind, do you see, your body has its own ego? It has its own attitudes. You have to succumb to it, isn't it? See, you say, "From tomorrow, I want to get up at five in the morning and walk on the beach." You set the alarm. The alarm rings. You want to get up but your body says, "Shut up and sleep." Doesn't it do it? It has its own way. So we start with the body. Hatha yoga is a way of working with the body, disciplining the body, purifying the body, preparing the body for higher levels of energy. All of us are alive; all of us are human beings, sitting here. But all of us do not experience life to the same intensity because our energy levels are not the same. Our pranic energies are not the same. Different people experience life in different levels of intensity.

For example, somebody sees a tree. A tree is just a tree. Most people don't even see it. Somebody sees the tree in more detail. An artist sees every shade of it. Somebody else not only sees the tree but also sees the Divine in it. Everybody sees. But seeing is not the same because the level of intensity with which you experience life is not the same. So we start with the body because that is something that you know. The whole process of yoga is to take you from something that you know and take the next step into the unknown. If you talk about something that you do not know, either you have to believe it or disbelieve it, isn't it? Suppose I start talking about God. You either have to believe my God or disbelieve my God, which will only take you into flights of imagination, not into growth. So now I talk about the body. This is something that you know. You know you have a body. Now you take the body to its peak. Now I talk about the mind. That is also something that you know. Take it to its peak and then the next step. You can only grow by taking the next step, the next step, and the next step from where you are.

Realizing where you are right now and taking the next step is growth. If you talk about something not known to you, you are only going into imagination. Imagination will run wild. Today all that is left in the name of religion are stories, stories and more stories. Now you don't know which is imagination and which is the reality. Yes? Many stories – story inside a story, and you don't know where the beginning is and where the end is.

So yoga starts like this – with the body, then the breath and then the mind. Now we have made this yogic science almost like a physical science. Suppose you mix two parts of hydrogen and one part of oxygen; you get water. Even when a great scientist puts it together, it is water. Even if an idiot puts it together, it is only water. Similarly, in yoga too, if you do this, this, and this, only this will happen. Whether a great yogi does it or an ignorant person does it, it doesn't matter.

If he does the practices and *sadhana* properly, the result is there to be seen.

So, in yoga, these systems have been identified. To start with, you work with the body, then you move to the breath, then to the mind, then to the inner Self. Like this many steps have been created. They are only different aspects. They are not really branches of yoga. In fact we address all of them at once. It is important that in a very balanced way all of them are addressed at once, as one unit. Otherwise, if you work just with the body, it is only preparatory in nature. So, there is really no division as such. Yoga is a union of all these.

Dynamic Stillness, Static Stagnation

If you look at it objectively, stillness and stagnation are about the same. Physically they could be seen as about the same, but qualitatively they are worlds apart.

Stagnation is a certain disease. It is anti-life. Stillness is a tremendous amount of life not manifesting itself in any way. It is just there – potent. That is God. God is stillness, not stagnation. The mind is stagnation. *Sadhana* is a force that moves you from stagnation to stillness, but between stagnation and stillness, when they are together, there seems to be very little difference, since your logical mind only understands in terms of moving and not moving. Not moving is stagnation, but stillness is also not moving. This non-movement, you may call it stillness or stagnation because it's purely subjective.

If you look at it objectively, stillness and stagnation are about the same. Physically they could be seen as about the same, but qualitatively they are worlds apart. A person who is meditating and a person who is sleeping may look about the same. One is sitting and sleeping, another is lying down and sleeping, that is all. For a person who doesn't know the difference, that's all he sees. Have you seen with how much sarcasm people look at meditation – those so-called dynamic people of the world? They think it's for people who don't even know how to sleep.

Externally there may be no difference between stillness and stagnation. Internally there is a tremendous difference. From stagnation to stillness, from ignorance to enlightenment, that's the difference. In a way, it is the same thing, only the quality has to change, that's all.

But how can you know the qualitative difference when you're drowned in ignorance? This is why the movement of sadhana has to go in full circle. Depending on how stupid a person is, that is how long the sadhana has to be. Physically and mentally, push yourself to the limit and see what is there. If you stop for every little discomfort, you will never know what it is. Just push yourself to the limit. Physically, mentally, emotionally, in every way push yourself to the last point, either you must go mad or you must get enlightened, that's all there is; and we will not allow you to go mad, don't worry.

That is why I keep asking you, "What is your priority? What is it? You have to increase it." Every time I ask that question, you have to push it up one more notch. To the point of discomfort you have pushed, but don't let up, push it up one more point and yet another point. It has to be pushed to the ultimate, to the optimum. Only then can the mind dissolve by itself. You don't have to do any other sadhana. This is the only sadhana needed. All other activity in the form of sadhana is just to get this one thing done. Make it in such a way that your *sankalpa* [1] is unshakeable.

Why someone is asked to go and live in the Himalayas for twelve years is not because if he lives in the Himalayas, the rocks could give him enlightenment. It is because he is even willing to waste his life for twelve years, with all kinds of hardship, just to seek Truth. If that kind of sankalpa has come, that man is very close. In a way, it is like literally wasting your life. When the whole world is eating well, drinking well and enjoying themselves, you are sitting there in the cold and chanting, "Shiva, Shiva, Shiva," knowing nothing might happen.

1 *sankalpa*: resolution

If you live there for long enough, you may come to know. Shiva probably will not come and bail you out. When you're hungry, you're plain hungry. When you're cold, you're just cold. You know it may turn out to be hopeless being there. In spite of that you stay, because the most important thing in your life is something else. When that sankalpa comes, it does not take twelve years. In one moment, it can happen. Nobody needs to wait for twelve years. This can be the moment. It is because you don't use this moment that you have to wait for the next one. This is always the moment. Are you going to tighten it up, or every time discomfort comes, will you think, "Oh, this is not for me?" It is definitely not for you if this is so. I am not saying the path is difficult, it's just that you make it difficult. The path is not difficult, it's very simple. If you are simple, it's very simple. If you are all wound up, the path is very, very winding. That's all it is.

This moment, when you're very simple and at ease, life is very simple, isn't it? When you're wound up, just see how complicated it is. Don't become all wound up. There is enough nerve-racking past in you, which is already in knots. Don't create new knots now. The old knots are already causing a lot of pain, causing a deep pit inside, which is eating you up in many ways. Some of you have become aware of this, and some are yet to become aware of that, but it is there in every human being. There is one empty pit within you which just eats you from inside. That is enough, isn't it? Don't create more now. What you have created in the past is enough. Many lifetimes of opportunities have been wasted, but this one need not go to waste too. Those of you who feel the urgency, please go on unrelentingly. To those of you who think, "Anyway, another ten thousand years are there, no problem," I am saying, "Why only ten thousand? There is a whole eternity ahead of you. There is no hurry. After all, what is wrong with life?" When I say it, it may look like a curse, but it is not a curse. I am saying, in this situation, when the energies are high like this, if you don't make use of this situation and me, if you don't see this, well then...

The Snakes &
Ladders Of Comfort

*Generally, mental alertness is mistaken for awareness,
but awareness is a far deeper dimension than just
mental alertness alone.*

The Snakes & Ladders Of Comfort

Whatever the past karma, it is like this: let us say, until the age of thirty you earn ten million rupees. Now you can either squander it or make it grow. In the past, you might have created some riches within you. In this life you may either add to it or squander it; but definitely some quality of that will be there in your life, though in unconsciousness it may go to waste. So because of your spiritual practices, those riches may manifest now in terms of material comfort, like a good house, the right kind of atmosphere, or maybe good people around you. In spite of all this, you may not make use of it and just become complacent. That is the whole cycle.

Why I repeatedly say that the whole game is like the Snake and Ladder game is: you climb the ladder and there you're happy. The very comfort that comes out of it, that comes out of good karma, may make you complacent and that is it – down through the snake you go. Then once suffering comes, you start looking and grow. You may squander it and go down again. This is the way of the fool, wasting his energy; but someone who has sufficient intelligence in him should even take each breath as a step towards growth. It is very much possible. Even after reminding a person hundreds of times, if he still does not wake up, if he is still lying down in his comforts, what can we do? He will be lost. He has to suffer once again, and then maybe seek growth.

This whole spiritual process is not happening to even one percent of the population. For all others, when things are going well they are laughing, and when things go bad they are crying. There are very few people in the world who, whichever way it is, are okay and balanced. For them nothing is a great benediction, nothing is a problem. Everything is just another life situation through which they can become free. The rest of the people are all the type who will go the way the situation pushes them. They are like cattle. You have evolved into a human body, but otherwise there is no real difference. Between the way animals live and generally the way people live, is there any great difference qualitatively? Maybe quantitatively there is a lot of difference. There is more variety to your activity; you drive a car, you watch television. All that nonsense you do, but qualitatively, where is the difference?

If the difference has to come, it can only come with awareness; there is no other way. Generally, mental alertness is mistaken for awareness, but awareness is a far deeper dimension than just mental alertness alone. When awareness arises within you, love and compassion will be the natural follow-up; then each breath becomes a step towards growth.

Life That Expresses Energy

*If you gain a little bit of mastery over your own energies,
you will see, things that you never imagined possible,
you will do simply and naturally.*

When we say "yoga", probably for many of you it means some physical postures – twisting yourself into some impossible postures. That is not what we are referring to as yoga.

Yoga means to be in perfect tune. Your body, mind and spirit and the existence are in absolute harmony. When you fine-tune yourself to such a point where everything functions so beautifully within you, naturally the best of your abilities will just flow out of you. When you're happy, your energies always function better. Do you see that when you're happy you have endless energy? Even if you don't eat, if you don't sleep, it doesn't matter; you can go on and on. Have you noticed this? So just a little happiness is liberating you from your normal limitations of energy and capability.

Now, yoga is the science of activating your inner energies in such a way that your body, mind and emotions function at their highest peak. When your body and mind function in a completely different state of relaxation and a certain level of blissfulness, you can be released from so many things that most people are suffering from. Right now, you come and sit in your office, and you have a nagging headache. Your headache isn't a major disease, but it takes away your whole capability for that day. Just that throbbing takes away everything. With the practice of yoga, your body and mind will be kept at their highest possible peak.

Life That Expresses Energy

There are also other dimensions to yoga. When you activate your energies, you can function in a different way. As you are sitting here right now, you consider yourself to be a person. You are identified with many things, but what you call as "my Self" is just a certain amount of energy. Do you know, modern science is telling you that the whole existence is just energy manifesting itself in different ways? If this is so, then you're also just a little bit of energy functioning in a particular way. As far as science is concerned, this same energy which you call as "my Self" can be here as a rock, lie there as mud, stand up as a tree, bark as a dog, or sit here as you. Everything is the same energy, but functioning at different levels of capability.

Similarly among human beings, though we're all made of the same energy, we still don't function at the same level of capability. What you call capability or talent, what you call your ability to do things in the world, your creativity, is just a certain way your energy functions. This energy, in one plant it functions to create rose flowers, in another plant it functions to create jasmine, but it's all the same energy manifesting itself. If you gain a little bit of mastery over your own energies, you will see, things that you never imagined possible, you will do simply and naturally. This is the experience of any number of people who have started doing these practices. It is the inner technology of creating situations the way you want them.

With the same mud that we build such huge buildings, initially people were building little huts. They thought that's all they could do with it. With the same earth, haven't we built computers? What you call a computer is dug out of the earth. We thought we could only dig mud and make pots or bricks out of it. Now we dig the earth and make computers, cars, and even spacecrafts out of it. It is the same energy; we have just started using it for higher and higher possibilities. Similarly, our inner energies are like that. There is a whole technology as to how to use this energy for higher possibilities. Every human being must explore and know this. Otherwise, life becomes very limited and accidental; you get to do only what you're exposed to. Once you start activating your inner energies, your capabilities happen in a different sphere altogether.

Yoga is a tool to find ultimate expression to life.

Do You Know
What You Don't?

*What you don't know, if you accept that you do not
know it, there will be growth.*

If the need to grow is deep within you, if that is your aim, first of all you should be clear about what is there in your experience and what is not. Clearly mark what is there in your experience and what is not. What is there in your experience, you know. What is not there in your experience you need not say it does not exist; just say: "I don't know." If you have reached this state, growth will happen by itself. What you don't know, if you accept that you do not know it, there will be growth. Instead, whatever you do not know you start believing in and think you know everything.

Now, if growth has to happen within you, you should see what is there in your experience right now. Right now, what is there in your experience? You have experienced your body to some extent, you have experienced your mind to some extent, and you have experienced the world to some extent. In some moments, you might have also experienced to a certain extent the energy which makes this body and mind function. Beyond this you have not experienced anything. Everything else is just imagination. Whichever way the society has taught you, your imagination is that way. Look into what is there in your experience and what is not. And all that is not there in your experience you accept as, "I do not know." This is very, very essential. Otherwise this whole life will pass in pretensions.

You don't have to come to any conclusion. What you do not know, if you accept as "I do not know," then the search will happen within. Whether it is God, whether it is truth, if you have to search, where should you search? You should search within, isn't it? If you have to search within, if you have to realize within, there is a need for the necessary tool, isn't it? Now, you have the urge to know the depth of the ocean. Is it possible to measure the depth of the ocean with a foot scale? You will come back with the conclusion that the ocean is bottomless. But that is not the truth, isn't it? To go inward, you need to have the necessary tool. What is there with you right now to go inward? What tool do you have right now? Just your five sense organs. You have nothing else to search. These five sense organs can realize only materialistic things. There is no chance of experiencing what is beyond the materialistic world with these limited tools.

Now this body is sitting here; this is very important right now. You have to feed it, you have to clothe it, you have to decorate it, and you have to do so many things to it. There is something invaluable within you and till now you have not experienced that. This something which is within you, if it goes away tomorrow morning, nobody wants this body after that. Even your city municipality does not want it after that.

Only because the fruit called life is inside this peel, this skin has so much value. What happens if the fruit within is gone? There is nothing after that. But you are not bothered about the fruit. You are very much occupied with the peel. If you keep on eating the peel all your life, how would it be? Bitter, isn't it? But the problem with the peel is that there is some sweetness here and there. Because of its association with the fruit, there is sweetness here and there. Now your whole life is about searching for that sweetness. If you struggle a lot, you will find some sweetness here and there. Instead of this, if you are able to realize the fruit beyond the peel, you can always be joyous. There is every possibility that you can be in this sweetness always. Had this peel been completely bitter, you would have all been enlightened by now. The trouble is, there is some sweetness here and there and you have gone after that sweetness and forgotten the very source.

The Choice Of
The Conscious

*If you have to do something that you do not like, you
can only do it consciously; there is no other way to do it.*

Everybody is making choices, but choices made in unawareness are compulsions. Let us say you get angry right now. It is your choice actually, to be angry. Somewhere, you believe that is the way to handle the situation, but the choice is made in such unawareness that it is a compulsion; it is happening compulsively on a different level. So you are living by choice, but choices are made without awareness – unconscious choices.

Now the whole thing is to shift into making conscious choices. Even a simple act, like when you wake up in the morning, the unconscious choice is that you don't want to wake up. When the sun rises, you want to pull the sheet up a little higher over your face. Do you see this? This is the unconscious choice. Your physical body wants to remain in the bed for some more time, and some more time, and some more time – for so many reasons, it doesn't want to get up.

There are so many aspects of life, so many limitations in your experience of life, that in many ways, unconsciously, you're not really looking forward to the day. Let's say tomorrow, you have planned to go on a picnic. Do you see, before the sun rises you will wake up on that day? Consciously you have decided the previous day; you are excited. You are looking forward to tomorrow. It is a joyful experience. You will see, you will wake up before the sun comes up. Otherwise, unconsciously, you try to pull the sheet higher up over your face because this light is not something you are looking forward to, because with light come today's stock prices; with light come today's problems; with light comes the whole world into your life. So you're trying unconsciously to screen yourself from that; but now we make a conscious choice. Even after you wake up, the unconscious choice is that you want to drink a cup of coffee, the body feels comfortable with that, but now you can make a conscious choice, "No, I will have a cold water bath and do my yoga asanas."

Why ascetic paths were set is simply because of this: you start doing things that are naturally not comfortable for you. Once you start doing such activity that is uncomfortable for you, you do it, but you don't like it. If you have to do something that you do not like, you can only do it consciously; there is no other way to do it. Yes? Things that you like, you can do compulsively; but things that you don't like, you can only do consciously. That is why the ascetic path. You start doing everything consciously. There is no other way to be.

Now, slowly, you are practicing how to be conscious in various situations in your life. When you are hungry, the natural urge is to grab food and eat. Now you make a conscious choice, "I am very hungry, but I am not eating." To stay away from food, there is no other choice except being conscious about it, but to go and eat, you don't need consciousness; you can simply go and grab it when you are hungry. These simple things are set up in life so that you start doing things more consciously. For example, we have only two meals in our day-to-day life, or sometimes even one meal. By the time this meal comes, naturally you are very hungry, but you don't immediately eat. You wait for everybody to sit down. You wait for something to go onto everybody's plate, then you utter an invocation, and then you slowly eat. This needs consciousness. Just to give that break when you are hungry – just to wait for those three or four minutes – it takes an enormous amount of awareness for a person.

So like this, you're cultivating awareness into different aspects of life. Maybe initially your awareness is only for half an hour a day, but gradually you are bringing awareness into various aspects of life like this. The idea of cultivating awareness is so that it slowly seeps into your life. In one way that is a reality, you are cultivating awareness. One thing it does is, it enhances the quality of your life, but that's not everything. The main aspect is that if you can maintain awareness in various kinds of situations in life, only then will you ever become capable of being aware at that moment when you have to part with the body. Otherwise, that never arises in your life.

Untie Those Knots

In your attempt to understand a flower, maybe you will pull it apart petal by petal. But you will understand nothing.

Most people don't know how to handle their life here. Do you see this in the world? Why are they pursuing life after death? What is the point?

Anything that is not in your experience, there is no way to understand and analyze. This needs to be extremely clear to every individual. People are always trying to understand life after death. You cannot understand anything which is in a different dimension than you are right now. The whole effort is to move to a different dimension. If that needs to happen, first you must stop understanding. You have to see that you cannot understand, and that there is no need to understand. It is the experience which takes you out of this dimension.

If you try to understand a flower, what will you understand? In your attempt to understand it, maybe you will pull it apart petal by petal. But you will understand nothing. Maybe you will know the chemistry of it. Maybe you will analyze everything and then you will conclude everything is proton, neutron, and electron. All that is fine, but you will not know anything about the flower.

Now people are trying to deliver spirituality as an understanding. Understanding is needed about how you are bound, that's all. You cannot understand the other dimension. See, people are always talking about how God is, how heaven is. This will not lead you anywhere except to hallucinations. The only thing that you need to understand is how you are bound to your limitations. If you understand this and free yourself from those bondages, where you have to go you will anyway go.

If I talk about the sky, it's no use. What are the ropes which are tying you down to the earth? That is all that matters. Your business is with the ropes that are tying you down, not with the sky. If you untie these ropes, you will anyway reach the sky. When you reach there, only then you will know what the sky is. Till then, whatever you think about it, whatever understanding, whatever analysis you make is coming from the limited dimension of where you are right now.

There is no way to understand that which is beyond your present level of experience. So the Guru's work is to help you to untie the knots with which you are binding yourself, and to show you where the knots are. And if you untie them and you're ready, you are on the edge; maybe just with one knot left, then he can push you. If he pushes you when you have ten ropes tied down, then it will damage you. He can push you only when everything is broken and just one single thread is hanging. Then he can push you. He can afford to push you because you will not break, only the thread will break. With yoga, you can mature the body, mature the mind, and mature the energies so that slowly, these bondages and ropes that we are tying around us gradually are broken down. A moment comes when all you need is a "Whoo!", you will go.

Spiritual Allergy

Unless you do something to the inner, you will not know what it is to be peaceful, to be joyous, you will not know how to go beyond the limitations of being just a physical body and mind.

Spiritual Allergy

It is very important that the spiritual dimension of life is brought into everybody's lives. Why many people have developed an allergy to spirituality is because somebody always told them, spirituality means leaving everything and going to the mountains. Even if you want to go, there is not enough space for all of you there. You had better learn how to be spiritual in your office, in your home, on the streets, wherever you are. You had better learn that, because spirituality is about your interiority, not what you do outside. Spirituality is an inner science to create a conductive inner atmosphere because the quality of your life is dependent on how you are within yourself. That quality this moment depends on how joyous, how peaceful you are. This dimension you have completely neglected. Unless you do something to the inner, you will not know what it is to be peaceful, to be joyous, you will not know how to go beyond the limitations of being just a physical body and mind.

See, your body is simply accumulations of what you have gathered from the earth — when you leave you can't take an atom of this body. So this body is not really yours. Your mind is not yours too. It is also just an accumulation — what you have gathered from the backgrounds in which you were brought up in life. So there is something else which needs to be looked at beyond these dimensions.

Even if I erase all your memory, still you will be here. Yes? Your family will disappear, your status will disappear, your business will disappear, everything that you own in the world will disappear. But still you are here. So beyond all the things that you identify yourself with, still there is something called as you. That you is not subject to what you accumulate from outside. But unfortunately that you has been so much covered, so much crowded with other things that you never allowed yourself to look at that. You always thought that what you are identified with is much more important than who you really are. Now if your focus shifts, then the other dimension can start opening up for you.

The whole process of spiritual science, yoga in particular, is to somehow elevate you to an experience that is beyond the five sense organs. When you transcend the limited experience of what you know as yourself, your experience of life is naturally in a different dimension. Then you begin to experience that which is not physical – the spiritual, the Divinity of your true nature. If you are ready and willing to experience life in a deeper dimension, to be truly happy, I have methods. Then you can begin to experience the joy, the blissfulness of knowing who you really are.

A True Prayer

A prayer is not a means to reach God, but God is only a
means so that we can pray.

The first question to ask is what is your prayer? "God, give me this, give me that, and save me." What you are seeking in prayer is not God, what you are seeking is free happiness. Ultimately what you want with prayer is well-being, you just are not willing to admit it. The first step is to be straight with yourself — then we can see how to cross the threshold of limitations to true happiness and well-being.

It is time that we realize that looking to God will not help until we look at our own foolishness. If you sincerely look at your deepest motivation for religion, you will see you have never aspired for the Divine. Please understand this. Your aspiration has never for the Ultimate. Your aspiration is for comfort, for wealth, for power, pleasure. And you think God is a tool to achieve all those things. When you are seeking protection or materialist things, greed and fear have become the basis of your prayer and this will not work.

Ordinarily, we think prayer is a means to reach God, but what do we really know about God? If we are truthful, we must admit we have no direct experience of God; we are coming from a particular belief system. The danger in using prayer to reach a God we have no direct experience of can be illusionary. Thoughts and prayer can open a person but at the same time they can create hallucinations. Once hallucinations start growing, they take on such a big dimension because the illusory is always more powerful than reality. An illusion has the freedom of becoming anything it wants.

A True Prayer

The cinema is more powerful than real life, given that you can just exaggerate it the way you want it. When the illusory process gets exaggerated, it becomes more powerful than life. That is why we have always stayed away from prayer because prayer can be not only misused but also deceptive. Meditation, compared to prayer, is a much more reliable method to reach the inner nature and experience the Divine.

Authentic prayer is a deep connection with the Divine inherent in everything and everywhere. It is a quality, a state of being. As we become prayerful it is extremely beautiful but that state is reached only when we connect to our inner nature. Then the experience is absolutely joyous.

When we are really joyous, we are wide open and can receive. Prayer no longer becomes a monologue, but a beautiful phenomenon and a celebration which brings great joy. Then we pray not out of fear or greed, but because prayer itself is the reward. Patanjali, considered the father of yoga, goes as far as to say that when one knows how to be truly prayerful, prayer is not a means to reach God, but God is only a means so that we can pray.

The Root Cause

If you truly become aware of the disease, then you become aware of the cause also.

The Root Cause

Physical existence is always happening between cause and effect. Suppose there is an infection, you ate or drank something somewhere and got infected; so the cause was bacteria.

Now there is an effect, infection. So you are trying to take away the cause by taking antibiotics. You kill the cause with medication, because it is external to you. With other diseases that are not externally caused, but are happening from within the body, the cause is so much deeper compared to an infection. For this type of disease to manifest, there is an imbalance or a malfunction in the energy body, which manifests itself in the physical body, or sometimes in the mental body.

Now with something like pranic healing − or any kind of healing for that matter − you are only appeasing the effect. In a way, what you are doing is that, with a little control or mastery over your own energies, you are able to put a screen between the cause and the effect. So the effect dies out, but the cause stays buried.

As far as nature is concerned, as far as life energy is concerned, the effect was only its way of telling you that there is a cause inside of you. What we call as "cause," the disturbance of energy, is trying to manifest itself in a certain way.

Let us say you have asthma and I just remove your asthma today. Without asthma in you, when you still have the same kind of energy in you, you may become some other calamity in a moment. The disease may not be there, but you could get into an accident.

Your asthma was only an indication of a deeper disturbance. If we take away your asthma, it may manifest in some other way, as some other calamity. This is because your energies are still in the same situation, but the effect of it was taken away. So, it will take effect in a deeper or more acute form to inform you again. Instead, if you bring awareness to your disease, you get connected to the cause of it.

When we talk about bringing awareness to your disease, when we talk about accepting what is there, it does not mean becoming defeated about your disease. If you truly become aware of the disease, then you become aware of the cause also. The moment you bring awareness to any part of your body, in terms of energy, it will immediately become active and many things start happening there.

Just as an experiment, if you carefully attend to any part of your body – put your attention there and just be with that, you will see that so much energy activity will begin to happen there, because if you bring awareness and consciousness to that part of the body, naturally life energies become enhanced. This way, one could heal something and change the energy situation to some extent.

Now, why did the energy body get disturbed, first of all? For the energy body to be disturbed either there is an improper lifestyle, improper thought patterns, improper emotions or a combination of all these. There is a certain karmic structure that you have built which is causing some kind of turmoil to your energy, which manifests itself in the physical body as disturbed energy or disease.

But even if you settle the energy situation to some extent with healing or mental focus or with a certain sense of awareness, still the karmic substance which is causing this is not gone. The karmic substance is recorded in your energy as the fundamental software. It can work only within the ambit of the programmed software.

The life energies within you created your whole body. All the bones, blood, flesh and everything, including your brain, were created by this energy. When you were born, your body was so tiny and today it has become so big. Nobody stretched you from outside, did they? Whatever is creating the body is within you. So, when it can do so much, can it not fix a tiny cartilage or a hole in the heart?

Now, this whole activity of trying to heal somebody is, in some way, trying to play God – trying to manipulate energies in an improper way.

Here, we are teaching people *yoga kriyas* with which healing happens naturally. The objective is not healing, but it definitely happens. This involves *sadhana*, which is dissolution of karma by itself. When the cause is dissolved, the effect is no more.

The War With Peace

Without being capable of bringing peace into your own being, there is no way you are going to be capable of bringing peace to the world.

Forces of love-compassion and anger-hate are always functioning in the world. It is a seesaw game. The question is, which end of the seesaw do you want loaded? If we are really on the brink of a terrible situation, it is all the more important that the spiritual process is applied more vigorously as ultimately that is the only thing that will maintain sanity in the world.

The moment you start believing in things that are not a living experience for you, you are naturally in conflict. Please see this. You are a peaceful person today, but tomorrow when somebody really confronts your belief system, you will stand up and fight.

What is the intelligence in moving into belief? What is the benefit of moving into belief? The only thing is your ego feels comfortable. "I don't know" is a big loss for the ego. "I know" is the only way you can make the ego grow, isn't it? In any given situation, when you say, "I don't know," you are incapable of fighting with anybody, you are incapable of conflict. You are a very humble and wonderful human being.

Without being capable of bringing peace into your own being, there is no way you are going to be capable of bringing peace to the world. If this little mind, you can't make it peaceful, are you going to make the world peaceful? Whatever you're seeing in the world is just a projection of your little mind, an enlarged projection of your mind. Is there anything happening in the world which is not happening in your mind? It is happening.

The science of yoga is a way to look inward. To look inward not from any standpoint, simply to look inward. You cannot look inward if you're identified with something. The moment you're identified, all doors are closed to you. Please see, the very way you think and feel depends on what you're identified with right now.

Let's say, for example, you identify yourself as an Indian. Now when a situation happens, the very way you feel and respond to it is in a certain way. At that moment, in national interest, maybe it's a good thing, but still, instead of reacting to it you can respond to it more intelligently. When you're identified, you just become a reaction. You have no choice to think any other way. You have no capability of seeing the other person's point of view. You have no capability of seeing from where the problem is springing. You will just react.

It is better that you come from your intelligence, not from your reaction. To come from intelligence, the first thing is you must be able to look at things just the way they are, not from an identity. The moment you look at anything from an identity, you are prejudiced about it.

Meditation is a way to help you drop your identity and experience true peace. At least when you sit and meditate, nothing else exists. There is just being, nothing else is there.

The War With Peace

Peace means nothingness. Peace is not something that you create. Peace is not something that happens. Peace is something that always is. Peace is the fundamental existence. What happens on the surface is disturbance. This is just like the ocean. On the surface of the ocean there's turbulence, but deep down it's perfectly peaceful. Only if you are in tune with that quality, you know true peace.

Flowers Of The Beyond

Choosing Your Destiny

Once you become a true individual, your destiny is yours.

Destiny is something that you have been creating unconsciously. You can also create it consciously. You can rewrite your destiny. All that we are doing in the form of spiritual process is just that. You decide where you want to go, taking the next course and destination. It is in your hands.

If you can touch that core in you, if you can for one moment experience that the source of creation is within you and shift your whole focus to yourself, you can rewrite your own destiny. All the time your focus is scattered, because what you consider as "myself" is your house, your car, your wife, your child, your pet, your education, your position, your power and your other identities. If I strip you of all these things, including your body and mind, which are just accumulations, you will feel like a nobody, yes or no? So what you call "myself" is spread around you right now.

When I say "you", it is you, not this carpet, not this wall, not your child, not something else. When I say "you", it's just you. If it shifts to this, you can rewrite your destiny whichever way you want. Right now, what is "you" is spread out; you are a scattered being. You are not an established being; you are a scattered being. You still have to gather all this mess, put it aside. Then it becomes you. You still have not become you; you are a crowd, isn't it? The crowd's destiny is always predestined. Once you become an individual – individual means, it comes from "indivisible". It cannot be divided anymore; it is this. It cannot be here and there. Once you become a true individual, your destiny is yours. I want you to understand this. Why in the spiritual process people who are in a hurry for spiritual growth are not getting into marriage, children and relationships, is because the moment you have a wife or a husband, you cannot help it; "me" gets identified with the other. Otherwise, they will not let you live, isn't it? Once you get identified with things that you are not, when that which you accumulated becomes you, in your experience, you get scattered.

That is how deep the bondage with the body is. It is the source of all attachments. You don't have to go on searching for non-attachment somewhere else. You don't have to go about distancing this and that in your life, but once you get scattered, your destiny becomes predestined. Whichever way your karma, it just goes that way. If you become an individual, the significance of *sanyas* [1] or *brahmacharya* [2] is just this: shifting your whole focus to you. When I say "you," it is just "you," not even your body or your mind. If you are unable to be like that, you just choose one more identity. When you say "you," make it "you and your Guru." You attach yourself to the Guru without any hesitation, because you have no entanglements from the other side. You can get as entangled as you want with him; he is not going to get entangled. The moment you are ripe, you can drop it. With other relationships, it is never so. If you get entangled, even if you want to become free, the other will not let you go. Either you can rewrite your own destiny or, if such awareness does not come, we can very easily rewrite destiny if

1 *sanyas*: renunciation; life on the path of the Divine towards Ultimate Liberation; the forth stage of life as per the Varnashrama Dharma

2 *brahmacharya*: lit. towards the Absolute; life of celibacy and studentship on the path of the Divine; the first stage on life as per the Varnashrama Dharma

you can just give yourself to me. So don't worry about the predestined thing. You just create a longing to grow, to dissolve, to know. What has to happen will happen. Why are you worried about all those things?

Once you become an individual, your destiny becomes yours. If your destiny is in your hands, will you choose bondage or freedom? What would you choose? Freedom, because the very longing of life, the deepest longing of every life is to become free, to become free from the very process that we refer to as life or death, to become free from that itself. So once your destiny is happening in awareness, the next step will just happen by itself, because life within you has the intelligence to choose freedom, not bondage. Only because your destiny is being created in unawareness, you go about weaving bondages around yourself.

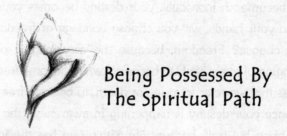

Being Possessed By
The Spiritual Path

*Every breath, every step, every act that you perform in
your life becomes a spiritual process.*

Once you are on a spiritual path, if you are genuinely on the path, you're not just obsessed; you are possessed. If you want to hit the peak of your consciousness, all the energy that you have has to be focused in one direction. If you're throwing it in ten different directions, it is obvious you are not going to get anywhere, isn't it? Even if you throw all the energy that you have in one direction, still it may not be sufficient. That is why the Master fills in that space of lifting you up when it is needed; but if you want to distribute your energy in ten different directions, then definitely it will be futile. So don't be obsessed; be possessed by the path. There is nothing else for you; everything else is just to get you there. Only when it becomes like this, your spiritual path means something.

If it is not so, if it is a side interest in your life, that you like spiritual entertainment – different people seek different types of entertainment and some people dabble with spirituality – that is up to you. I have nothing to say for such people. But if you're really seeking to know, then your whole being should be focused in one direction. You are completely possessed by it. This doesn't mean you will become unreasonable. This doesn't mean you can't run a family. This doesn't mean you can't fulfill your social responsibilities. Just use them as a spiritual process for yourself. Every breath, every step, every act that you perform in your life becomes a spiritual process. Only then there is no conflict. When you say, "This is my spiritual path, this is my family, this is my profession, this is my club, these are my drinking friends," then you have a conflict. If you eat, you eat only because you want to know. If you drink, you drink only because you want to know. If you work, you work only because you want to know. Then there is no conflict.

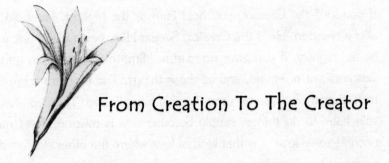

From Creation To The Creator

Let your humanity overflow and the Divine will happen.

If you love the Creator, you hold Him as the highest, you hold Him above creation. He is the Creator. Seeing Him, being with Him, would be the highest. If you have no trust in Him, then you talk in terms of existence, of no-mind, and all these things. The moment there is no trust, the whole issue becomes terribly complicated. Then you have to split hairs to do things, simply because love is missing. Trust means unconditional love. It is that kind of love where the other side need not respond. You simply love.

You must have loved like this when you were in school and college. The other side was not responding, but you went on loving. Once it happened, a young boy in college went to his professor and said, "I need your help." The professor said, "Sure, I am here to help you." The boy said, "No, it is not academic, it is something else." So the professor said, "Tell me." So the boy named the college beauty and said, "I am in love with her and I am fifty percent successful. For the other fifty percent, you have to help." The professor asked, "What do you mean fifty percent successful?" The boy replied, "Well, I am madly in love with her, but she hasn't responded!"

When a person has that kind of love that he does not expect the other side to even respond, it is okay. If God doesn't respond, it is okay. You have firm faith that he is there. Now look at this and see, we always love those who are not here. With most people it is so, they always love the dead, when they are not here anymore. When they were living, you couldn't look them in the face, you were not even on talking terms, but once they are dead you love them. You always love those who are not here, and it is the same thing with God. If he was here with you, if you had to share your food with him, if you had to share your life with him, then you would have had enormous problems with him, but because he is not here now, or at least not in your experience, it is easy to love him.

Love is not a joy; it is a deep wonderful pain. It is a very deep, tearing, wonderful pain. Something within you should tear; not just something, everything within you should tear. Only then you know what love is. If it feels pleasant, that is not love, it is just convenience. Maybe you felt a little affection. If you have ever loved, everything inside you tears apart, really tears apart. It is painful, but wonderful. That is how it is. When you start feeling like this about everything and everybody, then going beyond your physical and mental limitations naturally happens by itself. It doesn't happen by trying. If you try to go beyond your physical limitations with effort, you only injure yourself; but when it happens like this, it simply happens, physical limitations are no more limitations.

Some sage or saint might have talked about loving God, but now that you have a logical mind, a thinking mind, a doubting mind and a questioning mind, don't talk about loving God; it doesn't make any sense. The only reason you have started thinking about God or the Creator is because you have experienced the creation. Before you came, all that you call as creation was there, so you just assumed that somebody must have created it, and you started giving names and forms to that Creator.

So your idea of the Creator has come to you only through the creation. Now you hate the creation, you hate the person sitting next to you, and say that you love God; it doesn't mean anything. It will not lead you anywhere, because if you hate the creation, what business do you have with the one who created all this? Only if you have fallen deeply in love with the creation, then you have something to do with the one who created this. In the name of Divinity, do not forsake your humanity. Let your humanity overflow and the Divine will happen.

It is very significant that Jesus said, "Love thy neighbor." He doesn't mean falling in love with the person next door; he means just loving the one who is next to you right now, this moment, whoever it may be.

You don't know what evil could be happening in his mind; it doesn't matter whether he is good or bad, whether you like him or dislike him – just to love him the way he is. If you do this, then you merge with the creation. Once you merge with the creation, that is the only way to the Creator. Creation is the only way, or the only doorway to the Creator. If you reject the creation, you can't know anything about the Creator. So don't worry about loving God. See if you can bring love into your breath, into your step, into every act that you do, not towards anybody or anything; if you can just bring the longing to merge with everything around you, then creation will lead you on to the Creator.

What We Are Not

When a man has reached a state within himself where his actions are only to the extent required for outer life situations, then he is a complete person.

What We Are Not

First we need to know that the basis of our misery is that we have established ourselves in untruth. We are deeply identified with that which we are not. Somewhere along the way we have gotten identified with things around us. We have got identified with our body and mind. That is the source of suffering.

Whatever you have known right now, your experience is only limited to your five sense organs. Whatever you have known either of the world or yourself has come to you only by seeing, hearing, smelling, touching and tasting. If these five senses go to sleep, you will neither know the world nor yourself. They feel everything only in comparison. So this is not a genuine experience.

All yogic practices are fundamentally aimed at giving you an experience beyond the five sense perceptions. This is not in terms of physical reality, it is in a totally different dimension. That dimension, if you want to call it God, or if you want to call it my Self, it does not matter. Whatever your idea of God is, it is simply coming from the limited experience of who you are right now. It is not coming from any true experience. The only thing that you can experience is that which is within you. And that which is within you, you have never really looked at in real depth.

The whole experience of transcending your limitations must happen within you. If you want to transcend, only if you are truly willing, it can happen. Otherwise no power on earth or in heaven can move you.

Spirituality is simply the process of dis-identifying with what we are *not*, to shed the layers of conditioning so that we know what we are *not*. When that is completed, we arrive at something that cannot be discounted. This discovery will be the recognition of Divinity, and we will see that there is no reason for misery in the world.

The whole process of yoga is to make your interiority absolutely in your control. It is a possibility to move from a state of external enslavement to inner completeness, which is the state of unboundedness. If your inner nature is unbounded, your life is also unbounded. You can either sit with your eyes closed or you can perform different action — both ways your life can be complete.

When a human being has reached this state within himself, where his actions are only to the extent required for outer life situations, then he is a complete person. If within you, your inner nature has attained fulfillment regardless of the external situation, we can say that you have become unbounded. This is a state of true happiness.

Drop Your Limited Baggage Here

You deal with life as if you have got nothing to do with anything outside of your limited perception.

Spiritually, there has always been talk of surrender. But the moment logical, educated minds hear the word surrender, they will build forts around themselves.

In spirituality when the word surrender is used, it means you surrender that which is false. It is just that the very way you have existed up to now, is just a falsehood. What you refer to as yourself right now is simply a collection of identifications that you have taken in your life. Yet if you sincerely look at your essential Self, what have you got to surrender? You have nothing to surrender. Your essential Self is that which has always been and that which will always be. When you realize this fact, your spiritual work is done — you have already surrendered.

When you destroy the walls of falsehood that you have built, everything becomes one. In Truth, no walls exist in creation. You just believe they exist, so separation is your limited and distorted perception of reality. When you seek ultimate freedom, all that is required is the surrender of your illusions. And only when you surrender your illusions, reality happens. Reality, or Truth, is not right now in your experience. With all the multiple impressions that you have, you have built a world of your own. And this world is not real, it is not Truth. You cannot exist here for even a moment without interaction and contact with existence. But you go about believing you are a whole unto yourself. You deal with life as if you have got nothing to do with anything outside of your limited perception.

To drop these false boundaries is what the spiritual process is all about. This work does not have to happen in any particular way, with any specific process or person. For those who are willing to know Truth, there is always assistance. Spiritual masters simply create an atmosphere where it will become easier for a person to become free of his or her bondage.

Dropping identifications that you have carried for a lifetime is like jumping into the void – it is frightening. When you feel a presence that is bigger than yourself, it becomes easier to keep yourself, or what you think as yourself, aside.

Until you are able to keep yourself aside, there is no possibility of finding Truth. When you drop your limited identification, you no longer need to isolate yourself from the rest of existence. For a person who is seeking liberation, the only way to Truth is the destruction of all walls, which means the dissolution of your individuality. That is surrender, ultimate freedom, liberation.

Contemplate On The Highest

Whatever is your highest, you just contemplate upon that.
Your inner and outer purity will happen naturally.

You may have many great notions about yourself, but when you sit with me, all your deceptions are down and you stand stark. This is the very purpose of being with a Sadhguru. It is important that you realize the deception is on. So don't think; start looking. Don't use your stupid mind. It is the same nonsense. You cannot think any other way than you have been trained to up until now. Just look. The whole idea is to drop your stupid thinking. All this high and low, right and wrong is only in your mind. When you simply look at everything, everything seems to be okay. If you stand here and just look – the grass, the trees, the hill, the big mountain, the small mountain are all just part of the scenery. Does the cloud look better than the mountain? Or does the sky look better than the mountain? Everything is just a part of one unit. If you stand here and think, "this is a mountain, that is a cloud," then everything seems separate. The moment you project like this, all your nonsense, lifetimes of karma confront you. If you are simply here, looking at everything as it is, you become a different kind of a being altogether. You will mellow down to something totally different.

When you are in your mind, you don't travel anywhere. You only hallucinate. The first stanza of the Guru Pooja is just that:

Apavitrah, pavitrovā
Sarvāvasthāngatopi vā
yasmareth Pundari kāksham,
sabhahya bhyantara suchihi.

"Anyone – whether holy or unholy, whatsoever state he has reached – who meditates upon the lotus-eyed Lord, becomes sanctified both internally and externally." This means you are not involved in your own self-emancipation. You're not trying to improve yourself. You're not trying to purify yourself. You just contemplate on what you hold as the highest right now. Whatever is your highest, you just contemplate upon that. Your inner and outer purity will happen naturally. If you try to emancipate yourself, to improve yourself or to purify yourself, the more and more you do it, the more of a mess you will be. You simply contemplate on what you hold as the highest; maybe God, maybe the Guru, or whatever you hold as the highest. Or just contemplate on the sky; it is enough. Simply be with it, don't project God or anything on it. It is simply *smaran*. Smaran means remembering or contemplating on the highest. Now, everything changes, inner and outer purity naturally happen. Why temples are not working for people is because they are projecting about God. If they shift from projecting about God to smaran, there will be a tremendous transformation in them. People cannot remember God. If you have to remember, you should have seen Him somewhere or in something. Maybe in a child's face, your wife's face, your lover's face, maybe in a flower, in the clouds, somewhere you should have seen at least a glimpse of God; only then can you remember Him. Others can only think. Smaran means it has

happened. In this smaran everything is purified. Now you don't have to work on how to correct this or that, how to make this okay. Don't worry about all that nonsense. You just remember the highest aspect of life that you have seen. Just go on remembering that. That's your God for now. Everything can change out of that.

A Guru Mixes The Right Cocktail

*A live Guru mixes the right cocktail for you,
otherwise there is no punch.*

A Guru Mixes The Right Cocktail

Right now, the only things that are in your experience are your body, your mind, and your emotions. You know them to some extent, and you can infer that if these three things have to happen the way they are happening, there must be an energy that makes them happen. Isn't it? Without energy all this cannot be happening. Some of you might have experienced it; others can easily infer that for these three things to function, there must be some energy behind them. For example, a microphone amplifies sound. Even if you don't know anything about the microphone, you can infer that there is a source that powers it.

So these are the only four realities in your life: body, mind, emotion, and energy. Whatever you wish to do with yourself, it must be on these four levels. Whatever you wish to do you can only do it with your body, your mind, your emotions or your energy. If you use your emotions and try to reach the ultimate, we call this bhakti yoga; that means the path of devotion. If you use your intelligence and try to reach the Ultimate, we call this gnana yoga; that means the path of intelligence. If you use your body, or physical action to reach the ultimate, we call this karma yoga; that means the path of action. Now if you transform your energies and try to reach the ultimate, we call this kriya yoga; that means internal action.

These are the only four ways you can get somewhere: either through karma, gnana, bhakthi or kriya — body, mind, emotion, or energy. These are the only four ways you can work with yourself. It is just that in one person the heart may be dominant, in another person the head may be dominant, in yet another person the hands may be dominant; but everybody is a combination of these four. So you need a combination of these four.

It is just that, only if it is mixed in the right way for you, it works best for you. What we give for one person, if it is given to you, may not work well for you because that person is so much heart and this much head. Only when it is mixed in the right proportion it works for you. That is why on the spiritual path there is so much stress on a live Guru; he mixes the right cocktail for you, otherwise there is no punch.

There is a wonderful story in the yogic lore. One day, one gnana yogi, one bhakthi yogi, one karma yogi, and one kriya yogi were walking together. Usually these four people can never be together, because gnana yogi has total disdain for every other yoga; it is the yoga of intelligence. Normally, an intellectual person, a thinking person has complete disdain for everybody else. A bhakthi yogi, full of emotion and love, thinks all this gnana, karma and kriya yoga is just a waste of time. Just love God and it will happen. The karma yogi thinks that everybody is lazy and that they have all kinds of fancy philosophies; what needs to be done is work. One must work and work and work. The kriya yogi just laughs at everything. The whole existence is energy. If you don't transform your energy, whether you long for God or you long for anything, nothing is going to happen.

A Guru Mixes The Right Cocktail

So they can't be together, but that day they were walking together. Then it started to rain. They were in the forest and it started raining. They started running, looking for shelter, and there they found an ancient temple which just had a roof – no walls on the sides. In the center, there was a Linga. So these people went inside the temple for shelter. The storm became more and more furious and it started blowing in torrents. The fury of the storm was getting into the temple so they went closer and closer and closer to the Linga. There was no other way to be because it was just blasting them from all sides. Then it became very furious. There was no other place; the only way they could get some protection was for all four to hug the Linga. Suddenly they felt something enormous happening. A huge presence, a fifth presence was there. Then all of them said, "Why now? For so many years we have pursued You and nothing happened; why now?" Then Shiva said, "At last the four of you got together. I have been waiting for this to happen for a long time."

Without addressing the four basic ingredients of body, mind, emotion and energy out of which all your present experiences are rooted, one cannot move ahead. You can only start a journey from where you are right now.

A Guru Is A Live Map

To live on this planet, you need trust. Right now, you trust unconsciously.

A Guru Is A Live Map

Let us say all that you are seeking is to go to Kedarnath right now. Somebody is driving; the roads are laid out. If you came alone and there were no proper directions, definitely you would have wished, "I wish there was a map to tell me how to get there." On one level, a Guru is just a map. He is a live map. If you can read the map, you know the way, you can go. A Guru can also be like your bus driver. You sit here and doze and he will take you to Kedarnath; but to sit in this bus and doze off, or to sit in this bus joyfully, you need to trust the bus driver. If every moment, with every curve in this road, you go on thinking, "Will this man kill me? Will this man go off the road? What intention does he have for my life?", then you will only go mad sitting here. We are talking about trust, not because a Guru needs your trust, it is just that if there is no trust, you will drive yourself mad.

This is not just for sitting on a bus or going on a spiritual journey. To live on this planet, you need trust. Right now, you trust unconsciously. Let us say you are sitting in a bus, which is just a bundle of nuts and bolts and pieces of metal. Unknowingly, you trust this vehicle so much. Isn't it so? You have placed your life in the hands of this mechanical mess, which is just nuts and bolts, rubbers and wires, this and that. You have placed your life in it, but you trust the bus unconsciously. The same trust, if it arises consciously, would do miracles to you. When we say trust, we are not talking about anything new to life. To be here, to take every breath in and out, you need trust, isn't it? Your trust is unconscious. I am only asking you to bring a little consciousness to your trust. It is not something new. Life is trust, otherwise nobody can exist here.

So if you can draw your own map, if you can drive your own bus, that is wonderful. But on an uncharted path, if you go without a map, it may take lifetimes to find a certain place. It may take lifetimes to cross. If you go with a map you will cross easily. If you go with a good bus driver you will cross very easily; that's the difference. It is not that you can't do it yourself - you can. We don't know how long it will take. That is the question.

The Emperor Within

A spiritual person has earned everything else from within, only for food he begs.

To be spiritual means to be an emperor within yourself. This is the only way to be. Is there any other way to be? Consciously, would anybody choose to seek something from someone or something else? Maybe out of his helplessness he seeks, but consciously would anybody choose to do this? Wouldn't every human being want to be that way, where he is one hundred percent within himself? It doesn't mean you have to become totally self-sufficient. Always there is interdependence, but within yourself everything is there – you don't have to seek outside. Even somebody's company is not needed for you. If another person needs it, you will give it, but by yourself, you don't need anybody's company. This means you're no more a beggar within. Only for external things, maybe you will have to go to the world outside. This is ultimate freedom.

Spirituality is not for pussycats. You cannot do anything else in your life, but think you can be spiritual; this is not so. Only if you can take up and do anything in this world, then there is a possibility that you may be fit for spirituality, not otherwise. If you have the strength and the courage to just take up anything in the world and do it well, then maybe you can be spiritual. This is not for people who cannot do anything else. Right now, this is the impression that the whole country has – probably the whole world has – that only useless, good-for-nothing people become spiritual people, because the so-called spiritual people have become like that. People who are incapable of doing anything or people who cannot bear the ups and downs of life, all they have to do is to wear the ochre clothes and sit in front of the temple and their life is made. That's not spirituality. That's just begging in uniform. If you have to conquer your consciousness, if you have to reach the peak of your consciousness, as a beggar you can never reach there.

There are two kinds of beggars. Gautama, the Buddha, and people of that order are the highest kind of beggars. All others are plain beggars. I would say the beggar on the street and the king sitting on the throne are both beggars. They are continuously asking for something from the outside. The beggar on the street might be asking for money, food or shelter. The king might be asking for happiness, or conquering another kingdom or some such nonsense. Do you see, everybody is begging for something? Gautama begged only for his food, for the rest he was self-sufficient. All others, the only thing they don't beg for is food. For everything else they beg. Their whole life is begging. Only food they earn. A spiritual person has earned everything else from within, only for food he begs. Whichever way you think is better, be that way. Whichever way you think is a more powerful way to live, live that way.

Once it is like this, this person leads a different way of life. Once there is no hankering, once there is no need within him, only then he knows what love is, only then he knows what joy is, only then he knows what it means to really share. Now, sharing is, "You don't have to give me anything because I don't need anything from you, but anyway, I will share this with you." Setting up a whole life of barter may be convenient, but it is the way of the weak. This weakness is the first thing that has to go if you want to meet Shiva. If you want to meet Him, you better be on His terms. He is not going to come and meet a mere beggar. You either need to learn to meet Him on His terms or dissolve; these are the only two ways. Gnana and bhakthi mean just this. Bhakthi means you make yourself a zero, then you meet Him. Gnana means you meet Him on His terms – you become infinite. Otherwise, there is no chance of a meeting.

Love, or bhakthi, looks like a much easier path. It is, but there are more pitfalls on that path than in gnana. With gnana you know where you are going, you know if you fall. In bhakthi, you don't know. Even if you have fallen into a pit you will not know; that is the way it is. Even if you're trapped by your own illusions, you will not know. In gnana, it is not like this. Every step that you take, you know. Every step of growth, you know; every step backwards, you also know. I cannot say it is a hard path, but it's the path of the courageous, not of the weaklings. The weaklings can never make it, but everybody has the possibility of making it. Everybody has the capacity to do it if they rise above their limitations. It is just about whether they are willing to do it or not, that is all.

The way we think is the way we become. Whatever you hold as the highest, naturally all your energies get drawn towards that. A person who wants to walk the spiritual path has to make it that way in his mind that this is the highest, that "this is the first and last thing that I want in my life." So, naturally all his energies are oriented towards it. Only then the moment-to-moment struggle is gone and you don't have to struggle to correct yourself.

ISHA FOUNDATION

Isha Foundation is a non-religious, not-for-profit, public service organization, which addresses all aspects of human well-being. From its powerful yoga programs for inner transformation to its inspiring projects for society and environment, Isha activities are designed to create an inclusive culture that is the basis for global harmony and progress. This approach has gained worldwide recognition and reflects in Isha Foundation's Special Consultative Status with the Economic and Social Council (ECOSOC) of the United Nations.

Supported by hundreds and thousands of active and dedicated volunteers in over 150 centers worldwide, the Foundation's activities serve as a thriving model for human empowerment and community revitalization throughout the world.

Isha Yoga Center

Isha Yoga Center, founded under the aegis of Isha Foundation, is located on 150 acres of lush land at the foothills of the Velliangiri Mountains that are part of a reserve forest with abundant wildlife. Created as a powerful *sthana* (a center for inner growth), this popular destination attracts people from all parts of the world. It is unique in its offering of all aspects of yoga – *gnana* (knowledge), *karma* (action), *kriya* (energy), and *bhakthi* (devotion) and revives the *Guru-shishya* parmapara (the traditional method of knowledge transfer from Master to disciple).

The Center houses the architecturally distinctive Spanda Hall and Garden, a 64,000 sq ft meditation hall and program facility that is the venue of many residential programs. Also located at the Center are the Dhyanalinga Yogic Temple, Theerthakund, Isha Rejuvenation Center, Isha Home School and Vanaprastha for families. Isha Yoga Center provides a supportive environment for people to shift to healthier lifestyles, improve their relationships, seek a higher level of self-fulfillment, and realize their full potential.

Dhyanalinga Yogic Temple

The Dhyanalinga is a powerful and unique energy form created by Sadhguru from the essence of yogic sciences. It is the first of its kind to be completed in over 2,000 years. The Dhyanalinga Yogic Temple is a meditative space that does not ascribe to any particular faith or belief system nor does it require any ritual, prayer, or worship.

Within this architectural marvel, a pillarless dome structure, the vibrational energies of the Dhyanalinga allow even those unaware of meditation to experience a deep state of meditativeness, revealing the essential nature of life.

Every week, thousands of people converge at this unique meditation center to seek out inner peace and silence. Focal point of Isha Yoga Center, the Dhyanalinga is rapidly gaining in its global reputation as being one of the most sought out places for meditation.

Isha Yoga Programs

Isha Yoga programs allow individuals to take tangible steps towards their inner growth. These programs are designed by Sadhguru as a rare opportunity for self-discovery under the guidance of a realized Master.

An array of programs is conducted regularly by the Foundation worldwide. These programs establish optimal health and vitality, enhanced mental calm and clarity, and instill a deep sense of joy. They can be easily integrated into one's everyday life and embrace the human effort to reach inner awareness.

Action for Rural Rejuvenation

A long-time vision of Sadhguru, Action for Rural Rejuvenation (ARR) is a pioneering social outreach program. ARR aims at providing comprehensive and ongoing rural rehabilitation services, such as free medical relief, yoga programs, nature awareness programs, and community games to the heart of the rural communities of India, creating an opportunity for villagers, including women and children, to take responsibility for their own lives, and restore and reach their ultimate well-being. So far ARR has helped over 1.7 million people in more than 3,500 villages of South India (as at 07/2007).

Isha Vidhya

Isha Vidhya, an Isha Education Initiative, is committed to raise the level of education and literacy in rural India and help disadvantaged children realize their full potential. The project seeks to ensure quality education for children in rural areas in order to create equal opportunities for all to participate in and benefit from India's economic growth.

With English computer-based education, complemented by innovative methods for overall development and blossoming of each individual, Isha Vidhya Schools empower rural children to meet future challenges. Sadhguru's intention and goal is to start **206** English "Computer Friendly" Matriculation Schools within the next five to seven years, at least one in each taluk of Tamil Nadu. The schools are expected to benefit over **500,000** students when fully functional.

Project GreenHands

An inspiring ecological initiative of Isha Foundation, Project GreenHands seeks to prevent and reverse environmental degradation and enable sustainable living. The project aims to create **10%** additional green cover in the state of Tamil Nadu in southern India. Drawing extensively on people's participation, **114** million trees will be planted state-wide by the year **2010**.

As a first step, a mass tree planting marathon was held on **17** October **2006**. It resulted in **852,587** saplings being planted in **6284** locations across **27** districts in the state, by over **256,289** volunteers in just one day, setting a Guinness World Record.

Isha Rejuvenation

Surrounded by thick forests, at the tranquil foothills of the Velliangiri Mountains, Isha Rejuvenation helps individuals to experience inner peace and the joy of a healthy body. It offers a unique and powerful combination of programs, scientifically designed by Sadhguru, to bring vibrancy and proper balance to one's life energies. The programs contain a synthesis of allopathic, ayurvedic and siddha treatments, and complementary therapies, along with the sublime wisdom of ancient Indian sciences and spirituality.

All the proceeds of Isha Rejuvenation contribute towards providing free health care to rural villagers, under the Action for Rural Rejuvenation initiative.

Isha Home School

Isha Home School aims at providing quality education in a challenging and stimulating home-like environment, designed specifically for the inner blossoming and the well-rounded development of the child.

With its prominent international faculty and Sadhguru's personal involvement in the curriculum, Isha Home School kindles the innate urge within a child to learn and know. Focus is given to inculcating life values and living skills whilst maintaining the rigor of academic excellence as per national and international standards. It does not propagate any particular religion, philosophy or ideology, but rather encourages the child to seek a deeper experience and inner understanding of the fundamentals of life.

Isha Business

Isha Business is a venture that aims to bring a touch of Isha into the homes and environment of the community, and ultimately enrich people's lives. This opportunity is made available through its numerous products and services, from architectural designs, construction, interior design, furniture design and manufacturing, landscape design, handicrafts and soft furnishings, to designer outfits from Isha Raiment.

All profits from this venture are used to serve the rural people of India, through Isha Foundation's Action for Rural Rejuvenation initiative.

How To Get To Isha Yoga Center

Isha Yoga Center is located 30 km west of Coimbatore, at the foothills of Velliangiri Mountains which are part of the Nilgiris Biosphere. Coimbatore, a major industrial city in South India, is well connected by air, rail and road. All major national airlines operate regular flights into Coimbatore from Chennai, Delhi, Mumbai and Bangalore. Train services are available from all the major cities in India. Regular bus and taxi services are also available from Coimbatore to Isha Yoga Center.

Visitors should contact Isha Yoga Center for availability and reservation of accommodation well in advance of arrival to the center, as they are generally fully booked.

Contact Us

Isha Yoga Center
Semmedu (P.O.), Velliangiri Foothills
Coimbatore – 641 114 India.
Telephone: +91-422-2515345
Email: info@ishafoundation.org

Isha Institute of Inner Sciences
191 Anthony Dr.
McMinnville, TN – 37110 USA.
Telephone: +1-931-668-1900
Email: iiis@ishafoundation.org

Isha Institute of Inner Sciences
39 Barrier Point Road
London E16 2SB United Kingdom.
Telephone: +44-7956998729, +44-7939118981
Email: uk@ishafoundation.org

www.ishafoundation.org